Dancing
in the
Margins

Dancing
in the Margins

Meditations for People Who
Struggle with Their Churches

Kathy Coffey

A Crossroad Book
The Crossroad Publishing Company

"There is a secret medicine" and "Something opens our wings," by Jalal ud-din Rumi, were originally published by Threshold Books, 221 Dusty Ridge Rd., Putney, VT 05346.

The excerpt from "Among School Children" is reprinted with the permission of Simon & Schuster from *The Poems of W. B. Yeats: A New Edition,* edited by Richard J. Finneran, Copyright © 1928 by Macmillan Publishing Company, renewed 1956 by Bertha Georgie Yeats.

The excerpt from "Easter, 1916" is reprinted with the permission of Simon & Schuster from *The Poems of W. B. Yeats: A New Edition,* edited by Richard J. Finneran, Copyright © 1924 by Macmillan Publishing Company, renewed 1952 by Bertha Georgie Yeats.

The Crossroad Publishing Company
370 Lexington Avenue, New York, NY 10017

Printed in the United States of America

Library of Congress Cataloging-in-Publication Data
Coffey, Kathy.
    Dancing in the margins : meditations for people who struggle with their churches / by Kathy Coffey.
        p.   cm.
    Includes bibliographical references.
    ISBN 0-8245-1815-2 (pbk.)
    1. Church – Meditations. 2. Marginality, Social – Religious aspects – Christianity – Meditations.   I. Title.
BV600.2.C578 1999
242 – dc21   99-22091

1   2   3   4   5   6   7   8   9   10   04   03   02   01   00   99

For Michael Leach,
editor, publisher, and friend,
who thought of this book
and nurtured it with confidence
that even in pain we can join hands;
we can dance.

Contents

Part III
GREAT THIRSTS AND HIGH HOPES

Drumming the Rivers / 69

Well of Another Water / 78

Part IV
NURTURE AND HEALING

Of Spirits and Spines / 112

Part V
PARTNERS IN THE DANCE

Introduction

Maybe she's uneasy when good people are persecuted for apparently trivial reasons; maybe he's gay; maybe she groans inwardly every time she hears exclusive language in church; maybe he's a priest who follows Vatican II guidelines more enthusiastically than his local bishop's; maybe she's a minister who's been relegated to an isolated church; maybe he's divorced; maybe she's been fired from a youth ministry position because the kids spent more time serving at the soup kitchen than hearing lectures about the evils of premarital sex.

Maybe he's been fired after twenty years of service to his church and excellent evaluations; there is, of course, no due process. Maybe she finds herself in the awkward position of explaining to her daughter why she can't be a priest, but her brother can. Maybe he endures teasing from his colleagues at work for belonging to a church that violates many of the principles he believes in. Maybe after a painful divorce she comes to church and hears a homily that condemns her. Maybe his ministry to the elderly has been suspended because of one complaint from an extremist.

For whatever reasons, they've moved to the margins. At first, it's a painful place for those who once wanted to get it right, do good work, be sure and secure, help others, be at peace and at rest. Most of them were, at one time, the "good kids," the achievers, the award-winners, happy in following their calls, at home in their churches. They would never have envisioned themselves in the margins — leaving the prescribed paths and deviating from the approved scripts. Once at the heart of church life, they now stand apart. Their high expectations have shriveled; their influence or authority has dwindled.

For those who come to the margins bitter and aching, this land is a place of exile, what Jeremiah called "a lava waste, a salt and empty earth" (17:6). They feel betrayed by people and a system

11

that were important to them, a church that they once honored. Now it has either viciously turned on them or blithely ignored them. What they revered has become empty, hypocritical; they feel mortally wounded or numbly indifferent. People they once respected as leaders and mentors have become enemies. Their own gifts and talents have been tossed into the dust with a cavalier lack of concern.

They are stunned by the irony: that the community which should honor the gospel betrays it, that those who should resist the sexism, ageism, homophobia, exclusion, racism of the larger culture instead reinforce it, that the followers of Jesus who should shout a resounding "No" to injustice instead whimper acquiescence. They worry that all the good the church is capable of doing seems at times to get lost in trivia, smothered by a rigid preoccupation with orthodoxy. The "Yes" that should sound clearly, as clarion to a hurting world, whispers, muffled and diminished.

Others may gravitate toward the margins more from mild dissatisfaction than from bitter pain. Perhaps they have been patronized or ignored; perhaps their thinking has outgrown or deviated from their church's official line. They may feel discontent with rituals that once inspired, but now fail to nurture. Within this group are young people who feel dismissed because their voice has little effect on the shaping of church policy.

So in pain, confusion, or indifference, with clarity, conviction, or a "who cares?" shrug, those who struggle take a step back, a step into the margins. For many it is a life-giving move. There, they meet others who have been ignored, diminished, belittled. There, the reassurance of the marginal community sounds clear: "You're not alone, and you're not crazy." That message may even be phrased as the elegant invitation of the adage: "as long as we're walking on thin ice, we might as well dance!"

Why dance? It's an abnormal response to an abnormal situation — under the circumstances, perfectly appropriate. Without argument, without confusing words or mixed signals, the dance affirms what we know at the deepest level: that far beyond the surface turbulence abides a loving God. In God's steady arms, we rejuvenate, transform, heal, try a few wobbly dance steps.

Within the circle of God's embrace, we hear beneath the surface cacophony a lovely music. God calls us to plunge deeper and to move on, gracefully.

The responses to God's invitation vary because people are at different places in their struggle. Some may think the *last* thing they want to do is dance; they'd rather curl into a fetal position. Others may begin with learning a few tentative steps. One step might be recognizing the huge difference between God and the church, as Dorothy Day once did: "I loved the church for Christ made visible. Not for itself, because it was so often a scandal to me. Romano Guardini said the church is the cross on which Christ was crucified."[1] For those who once equated God with the church, it is a startling breakthrough. But in the long run, most Christians come to realize it's God who is holy, not necessarily the church. The church is filled with human beings, and hence with human cussedness, blessedness, pain, contradiction, and agony.

Others may eventually lead the dance, as they learn to extract what is life-giving from their tradition and let go of what is death-dealing. They master the skill of resistance, and they in turn bring life to others. When a friend says, "I've just been fired after fifteen years of service to my church because I have asthma," they can become healing balm. They bring the compassion of one who has been there and can offer genuine empathy.

Over time, they may discover the margin is the preferred place to be. Richard Rohr puts it bluntly: "If the system is a mess, those outside of it are at a significant advantage!"[2] It is not the first time the margin has become the place of justice and grace. There, Jesus spent most of his time; there, he touched and healed and welcomed all who were ostracized, for whatever reason, by the social-political-religious community. There, people still find him.

A gospel parallel for this situation might be the disciples caught in a storm at sea. They panic, but Jesus remains unperturbed, asleep on a pillow in the boat. Robert Barron describes the scene:

> The sleeping Christ stands for that place in us where we are rooted in the divine power, that soul space where, despite all of the vagaries and dangers of life, we are one with the God

who governs the whole cosmos and whose intentions toward us are loving. Even when every aspect of my person is agitated and afraid, that central place is peaceful, at rest. Of course, we see that Christ, once awakened by the disciples, rebukes the winds and calms the waves. This means that the source of peacefulness in the whole of one's person, the spiritual power that can restore calm to the stormiest life, is the inner Christ, the ground of the soul.[3]

To that inner center we turn — a graceful pirouette that may be the first of many dance steps.

This book begins by exploring in Part I three "whys?":

- Why dance?

- Why meditate?

- Why the margins?

The sections that follow describe movements that with some imaginative stretching might be considered dance steps:

- Part II — reaching a turning point

- Part III — plumbing the inner depths

- Part IV — finding nurture and healing

- Part V — remaining partners with God and each other

Each section contains similar components: a biblical model, poetry, people's actual experiences, questions for reflection or discussion. The interplay between the scripture, the person's true story, and the reader could create a dance of its own. Each personal story in itself could be a meditation. The people (all with fictitious names) who describe their struggles are sometimes conflicted, sometimes inspiring. They offer vibrant proof why "the New Testament does not expend energy describing the body of the resurrected Jesus, but it lists the primitive community of saints by name (Acts 1:12–14)."[4] In them, the body of Christ lives on.

Some wrestle with a specific issue, such as church teaching on gay/lesbian issues or birth control; others counsel people wounded by church; others perceive narrowness or injustice or simply know that something is seriously wrong. But each has discovered a way of coping and going forward that, in keeping with the metaphor, might be termed a unique dance step.

But before the dance, the history. For the invitation to dance is an invitation to participate in an ancient and sacred ritual. More background follows in the next chapter....

– Part I –

Three "Whys?"

O body swayed to music, O brightening glance,
How can we know the dancer from the dance?

— W. B. YEATS, "Among School Children"

It may seem an odd way to struggle with churches: to dance in the margins, to meditate. This section explores each of the three responses. "Why Dance?" gives a background on the history of dance. Through a poem and story of the Canaanite woman, "Why the Margins?" seeks to understand what the margins meant to Jesus. "Why Meditate?" proposes that the inward journey offers all we need to resolve the outward struggle. In the story of Laura, a dancer and minister, all three themes coalesce; theory becomes reality.

1

Why Dance?

Why dance? Because God is good, because life in all its craziness is full, because we have zest and energy and joy, because it praises God. God in turn must delight in the sight of beloved creatures moving in harmony, with the dignity, grace, and flexibility intended at their creation. Usually, people dance freely in social settings where they aren't trying to earn a paycheck or win an award. It is the uninhibited motion natural to children. While our limbs are still flexible and our bodies can still move, however stiffly, we dance to celebrate being alive.

Furthermore, we dance in imitation of our God. Nietzsche said he could believe only in a God who would dance.[5] Contemporary theologians like Elizabeth Johnson and Robert Barron compare the relationships within the Trinity to a constant flow, a rhythmic play of self-forgetting love, giving and receiving. From such classics as Thomas Aquinas and Augustine, Barron teases the implication: "We find our joy inasmuch as we imitate the divine dance."[6]

While most of us don't aspire to careers in dance, the professional performance can teach much about dance in less perfect forms. Dancers who epitomize freedom and beauty also model discipline and precision. Underlying the explosive celebration is careful choreography, long planning, and practice. The audience may get caught up in a swirl of color, passion, rhythm, and intensity. The dancer knows not only the zest, but the deliberate work and commitment. For the pattern of the whole to come together, each individual must play a perfect part.

Dance Partners

The relationship between the part and the whole leads to another question: with whom do we dance? Anyone asked by another person to dance may react in various ways: with reluctance, with exuberance, with stalling — "let's wait for a slow one" — with worry about getting the steps right. The same responses may come into play when the dance partner is divine. Or as Joyce Rupp points out, hesitation may turn to "great joy at being asked because you have long wanted to dance with this Partner."[7]

For those who can imagine the life of faith as a dance with God, it colors our whole spirituality. If we dance with God, it doesn't much matter where we dance. If the divine partner shifts slightly beyond the polished surface of the ballroom, who's complaining? With someone so accomplished, we learn to trust the moves. We can still dance gracefully — outside, on porch, patio, or deck, on the fringes of the crowd. Perhaps it is less important where we dance than that the dance continue.

Primitive Dance

For the long, rich history of dance deserves to go on. Reclaiming the metaphor of dance is important in light of the fact that "perhaps the greatest disservice that formal religion has rendered to our world is its tendency to disrupt the dance."[8] Scholars have shown that dancing is a deeply rooted human instinct. Our earliest ancestors danced to communicate with each other, with nature, and with God.

People disenchanted with formal religion may be heartened to know that primitive peoples *danced* their relationship to the divine. "Primitive religion is not believed. It is danced," says Arthur Darby Nock, the Harvard historian of religions.[9] Another scholar concurs: "Long before religion was ever taught, preached, or codified in sacred texts, it was lived and celebrated in ritual play and dance."[10] Now we term one particular dance form used in worship "sacred dance." Then, all dance was sacred, a dance with creation.

That exuberant and spontaneous ritual explored the meaning of human life. But over time, it disintegrated into "structures without a spirit, insipid formalities devoid of feeling and imagination."[11] If that was the effect of formal religion on the dance, then it is appropriate that efforts to reclaim the dance come not from the institution, but from the margins. Those excluded from official circles are the most likely candidates to create new forms. Leaders who control innovation are less likely to appreciate the brand new wonders that can arise from confusion.

Old Testament: Dance as Metaphor

Two Old Testament figures learned in unusual places that chaos can be a place of birth. A dry valley filled with dead bones seems an unlikely place to dance. Yet people exhausted from a long struggle can easily identify with Ezekiel's vision of the Hebrews who say, "Our bones are dried up, and our hope is lost; we are cut off completely" (Ezek. 37:11). God opens their graves, breathes upon them, and gives them the spirit of life.

One can only imagine the rattle and clatter, the clanking and dipping and bending and lurching of the crazy dance as bones come together, sinews grow, flesh and skin cover them. The scene may recall memories of Halloween skeletons dancing to songs about dry bones, but the biblical reality tops any fiction. "And this," says our God with a smile and a wave, "is the dance to which I invite you."

If such an invitation makes us want to laugh uproariously, we're in good company. That's exactly how Sarah responded when God drew her into an unusual dance. She shouldn't have been surprised. In her youth God had led her far beyond the comfortable borders of her own country and the coziness of home. She had left safety in Ur of the Chaldees to pursue a promise, a wisp of a blessing. She and Abraham had followed a God who danced before them with visions of descendents numerous as the stars or the grains of sand on the shore. That music was hard to resist; they turned the desert to dance floor.[12]

But that was in their youth. In old age, they could barely remember the song, and they grew too creaky and arthritic to dance. So the God of surprises announced an offspring. Abraham "fell on his face and laughed" (Gen. 17:17). Sarah, who was eavesdropping behind the tent flap, laughed (Gen. 18:10–12), and they named their child Isaac, or "laughter." As one commentator says,

"At that moment when the angel told them they'd better start dipping into their old-age pensions for cash to build a nursery, the reason they laughed was that it suddenly dawned on them that the wildest dreams they'd ever had hadn't been half wild enough."[13] All sorts of lovely dances can happen on the margin; in fact, it's a more likely place for improvisation than the corridors of power.

Contemporary Dance

Contemporary thinkers also bring their lenses to bear on the subject of dance. Thomas Merton wrote that every miniscule part of life was part of the sacred movement of God at play in the world:

> The Lord plays and diverts Himself in the garden of His creation, and if we could let go of our own obsession with what we think is the meaning of it all, we might be able to hear His call and follow Him in His mysterious, cosmic dance. . . . For the world and time are the dance of the Lord in emptiness. The silence of the spheres is the music of a wedding feast. . . . No despair of ours can alter the reality of things, or stain the joy of the cosmic dance which is always there. Indeed, we are in the midst of it, and it is in the midst of us, for it beats in our very blood, whether we want it to or not. . . . We are invited to forget ourselves on purpose, cast our awful solemnity to the winds and join in the general dance.[14]

The discoveries of quantum physics and theology have fine-tuned the idea that God's activity undergirds the constant motion and expansion of the universe. The life force itself may be a kind of music, to which all creation dances: from planets to subatomic particles. The patterns of dance parallel the symmetries discovered by scientists who study structures not visible to the naked eye.[15] God is revealed in intricate details which relate harmoniously, "the variegated and diffuse shapes that nature dances into being."[16]

Theologian Diarmuid O'Murchu explains that the desire to dance "has become a powerful metaphor to understand and explain the nature of planetary and human life."[17] "We can conceive of a universe in which the spheres themselves are dancing."[18] Such knowledge, rather than being too esoteric to influence us, may instead "enable us to engage more meaningfully in the dance of life and understand afresh the creative energy at the heart of our quantum universe."[19] We play a part in a dynamic and creative process, participants in an elegant dance.

Finally, a professional dancer contributes a personal answer to the question, "Why dance?" Kateri Caron says: "In the beginning, dance for me was a way to dress up the liturgy, an adornment. I have become less and less able to do that. I have come to believe that dance is among the arts that help us examine something deeper. Dance reaches to a level of the soul our words can't reach."[20] For her it is another way to pray. It may also become that for us, bringing music to the struggle, enriching our steps with poise and grace.

Your turn:

- How do you respond to the image of the spiritual life as a dance with God?

- How do you see the invitation to dance with God? As a risk? a challenge? a gift?

2

Why Meditate?

If we define meditation as a churchy activity, then it may be the last thing people struggling with church would want to do. If, however, we explore a broader definition, meditation is the only activity that can sustain and resolve the struggle. Consider the alternatives: talking with friends creates empathy; yelling, screaming, and pounding on walls vents anger; exercising relieves stress. But all of these solutions — like others that are unnamed — remain at the level of struggle and may in fact endlessly replay and extend it. None go inward, where thorny issues may be resolved.

Perhaps it helps to visualize a stream. On the surface float dead leaves, twigs, various flotsam and jetsam. At that level the stream may appear muddy or murky; it is hard to see further down. But at the level below the surface, the water clears and fills with sunlight. The mystic Mechthild of Magdeburg found this true, as did many other saints: sinking deeper, going inward restores vision.

So it is with prayer: the greater the surface disturbances, the deeper we must seek clarity. As a situation worsens, we need prayer more. We may thrash wildly on the surface, casting about for other solutions. One more analogy: when the outer journey grows rocky, we must pursue the inward journey.

While some might criticize the reflective route as escapist, it is the way to serenity. As a spiritual practice it has been tried and proved effective by seekers over the centuries, who contended with situations sometimes far worse than our own. It is also the way of Jesus.

Jesus' Habit of Prayer

When we look to the gospels, we find a record that his habit of meditation is constant. Never does he say, "Today I cured disease, multiplied loaves and fishes, confronted the Pharisees and raised the dead. I'll get to bed early — no need to pray!" Instead, his constant prayer keeps him in touch with his deepest identity as the beloved child of God. At the beginning, at the end, and throughout his ministry, the refrain recurs: "Jesus withdrew to a deserted area to pray."

This pattern in Jesus' life shows us that we too can constantly begin again, no matter how far into a rut we may have descended. John Shea reminds us that the words spoken at Jesus' baptism — "You are my beloved. In you is my pleasure" — are repeated to us at every moment.[21] The realization that he is loved energizes Jesus; reflecting on it in long silence can also convince us. "Could it be true that every time we realize we are the beloved filled with the pleasure of God, we begin?"[22] Even when we're exhausted, we think we have no more to give, or we despair that things will ever improve, this reflection can spur us onward.

Throughout his ministry, prayer continues to empower Jesus. The disciples, notoriously dim-witted on other aspects of Jesus' ministry, nevertheless recognize how prayer grounds his work. In contrast to their own fumbling efforts, he is clear, centered, single-hearted; people are drawn to his compassion. Wanting to be like him, his followers see in him the possibility of their own transformation. "We too could be like Jesus," they sense — and the key to change seems to be prayer. Hence, their request that leads to learning the Our Father: "Lord, teach us to pray." He introduces them to an inner work which John Shea calls "a series of inner adjustments, attitudinal alterations" that enable God to work more potently for good.[23]

At transitional times and before crises, it is not hard to predict what Jesus will do. Forty days of prayer in the desert preceded his public ministry; the prayer of Gethsemane prepared him for his passion. Before he calls Lazarus forth from the tomb, he looks upward and thanks God (John 11:41). John records that before Jesus washed feet, shared the last supper, and gave himself in bread and wine, he was firmly grounded: "Jesus, knowing that the Father had given all things into his hands, and that he had come from God and was going to God..." (13:3).

Meditating on that line alone should put all our dilemmas into a different light. If we have come from God and go to God, obstacles in the way are minor; anything that looms too large can be reduced to scale. What could be more important than that identity which God secures? Especially in the context of the suffering and crucifixion that will follow, the passage reminds us that nothing can interfere with our passage through this life into God.

From Prayer to Service

Immediately afterward, Jesus takes up a towel. We use a towel for wiping up spills, drying dishes or bodies after a shower, all practical, simple needs. When Jesus takes it up, the towel becomes the banner of a new order. In the reign of God, inflated titles and pompous attitudes carry no weight. Privilege and power have been replaced by service. If our churches have lost that notion, they have gone too far from their founder. Perhaps it is our task to take up the towel again, leave the shouting matches and the angry politics behind, resume service to a world that desperately needs it.

Admittedly that is harder to do if we've been scarred or wounded in the struggle with church. The old adage is correct in saying "hurt people hurt people." What can break the vicious cycle? Only a step out of the ring; only the path that transcends; only the power of God which we contact not by screaming or shouting, but by entering into a silence full of presence, a presence from which no one is marginalized.

Your turn:

- When in the past has meditation been for you a refuge, a place of empowerment, a force to energize your service to others?

- Can you turn to meditation now as a source of strength in your struggle? Why or why not?

A Canaanite's Terrain

He is exhausted: the crowds grabbing and greedy,
the roads dusty, shrill voices poking and jabbing.
John's brutal murder still raw, the sadness sharp.
Weariness a burdensome cloak on aching shoulders,
while the relentless Pharisees test and prod.

Faces in the crowd blur; he seeks the solitude of
borderlands. In Tyre and Sidon he hunts for
peace, and finds a shrieking woman who will not
hush. One more clamoring need in the din; he turns
away, searches the inner island secure from her shout.

Officious protectors, the disciples urge him to
flee the furthest reaches of her annoying voice.
They draw walls around him; he protects himself
with a mission focused, clear: Israelites only.
Heavy and black, the border line shuts her out.

She bangs clenched fists on the locked gate; she
will not be barred. Driven by beloved memory,
the agony contorting her daughter's face, her
once graceful gesture twisted, jerking, spastic.
He is not the only one who's tired, worn by long pain.

Their conversation like grenades launched between the
trenches, interrupted by a pirouette, a pause: her humor.
Crumbs tossed from the table, dogs snuffling the floor.
She overturns his gravity, tickles his fatigue. He laughs;
the borders blur; the kingdom mapped larger than he thought.

3

Why the Margins?

Some move to the margins because they've been driven out by the establishment; others go freely, recognizing there the locus of life. For others it may not be a major, conscious choice, simply a gradual movement because they act or think differently from mainstream churchgoers. The lure of a different drummer can sound as strong for us as it did for Thoreau.

For disciples of Jesus, the move to the margins follows his lead. He spent much of his time in the margins; for him they were a fruitful place. Let's take one example, Matthew 15:21–28. The setting of the story is the symbolic tip-off to what follows: Jesus is strolling the borders of Tyre and Sidon. The woman he meets there is caught in another set of borders, between disease and health. She is already marginalized; if she were ensconced in polite society, she would not shout with such loud desperation, would not plead so avidly for her daughter, troubled by a demon.

Where we would expect the usual outpouring of generous healing in response, Jesus ignores her. Jesus seems paralyzed; the sentence describing him sounds stark: "But he did not answer her at all" (Matt. 15:23). It's as if abruptly the music halts; the silence falls. Such nonresponse from Jesus is puzzling. Mere marginalization has never bothered him before. Most of the people he befriends and heals are marginalized.

Apparently what troubles him this time is his self-concept, the way he has defined his mission: to the Jews alone. She invites him beyond those narrow borders to a larger world. Perhaps she awakens a memory: his mother had told him of mysterious visitors from distant countries who attended his birth and heralded this wider world. The pesky woman wants to lead him further than the arena for his ministry as it has been traditionally defined. He hesitates because she asks him to dance in the margins.

Jesus' Turning Point

At stake is his whole identity; he must rethink his most basic assumptions. Invited beyond his culture, what he has conceived as his mission, everything familiar, he pauses as any human would. It all hangs precariously balanced as if on a scale: on one side, everything he and his parents held dear. On the other, a strange new call to something he hadn't anticipated. The Hebrew people, their history, religion, and culture had been his whole world. He'd been taught to scorn the Gentiles. If he responds to this one woman, will he open the floodgates for thousands more? He cannot foresee that the Jews will remain a small part of the larger history of Christianity. He has no crystal ball to predict how Gentiles will embrace and spread the faith worldwide. It's a wonder he doesn't hesitate longer.

When the conversation does resume, it is a dance with words. Through parry and thrust, word play and verbal jab, Jesus and the woman needle, tease, and finally reach a breakthrough. For Jesus, the turning point comes with the vehemence of what we might call a "slap-to-forehead" moment: "Woman, great is your faith!" (v. 28). He has a sudden appreciation for his new dance partner. The kingdom *is* larger than he'd thought; saving grace can spill over the traditional barriers. When a mental block to God is removed, the divine power flows freely and the woman's daughter is instantly healed. John Shea points out that "we are border people, touching divine love and human reluctance simultaneously."[24] Surely this story demonstrates the innovations, the surprising turn-arounds, the amazing cures that can come in the margins. If we follow Jesus, we should turn to such zones with anticipation.

Human Hesitation

But because we are human, we hesitate as he did. Many of us grew up with clear definitions of right/wrong, in/out. Most experts believe that children need well-defined parameters in which to flourish. For those who are developing a sense of what's wrong and what's right, consideration of the gray areas isn't helpful. It is only over time that we come to appreciate all the areas not covered by the lines of demarcation and the zones that were so clear to us as children.

Our positions bend and our thinking changes as we meet fine people who, for whatever reasons, don't color inside the lines — or we step outside them in various ways ourselves. At first it's confusing, but most people learn, mature, and, like Jesus, discover that the boundaries we thought were fixed are in fact fluid. We also discern what we hold sacred, and which beliefs aren't worth the battle. Ask mature people how their stands on certain controversial issues have changed over a period of twenty years. They'd probably be the first to admit how positions are modified and refined.

Still, none of us remain immune from the negative aspects of overcertitude. Where do we still draw the hard, fast lines? What other people or what part of ourselves do we exile or exclude? On what issues are we still uninformed or prejudiced? Where do we need to look again at Jesus as a model of learning, at his preference for compassion over purity?

A final passage about growth and maturation bears reflection:

> In that renewal there is no longer Greek and Jew, circumcised and uncircumcised, barbarian, Scythian, slave and free; but Christ is all and in all! (Col. 3:11)

If we were to rephrase this in contemporary terms, it might be: "There is no longer native-born or immigrant, male or female, ordained or lay, educated or illiterate, in communion or excommunicated, sanctioned marriage or 'irregular' one, approved or not, imprimatured or banned. In each of you flows the divine power; Christ calls you to be greater, more, all that he was!"

Your turn:

- What have you learned in the margins that you haven't learned in the approved, central places?

- Can you recall a "slap-to-forehead" moment in which you had a realization such as Jesus had, that the world was larger than anyone suspected?

4

Choreographing the Themes

L A U R A

If anyone's story combines our three themes — why dance? why meditate? why the margins? — it is Laura's. To see her doing liturgical dance is to experience grace in a new form. She dances not because it is cute or pretty, but because it is the only movement that gives proper dignity to God. While the dance may seem ethereal, Laura is rooted in the realities of struggle and resistance. Perhaps this foundation gives her dance its strength.

Ordained a minister in the Disciples of Christ, Laura has worked in a Lutheran hospital and a United Methodist church. Currently she teaches liturgical dance and heads her own dance troupe. But that story is better told in her own words. No romantic, she plunges at once into realism:

Dancing Tragedy

"I almost didn't teach Monday night, because I was devastated by the funeral Monday morning. A dear friend had died at age forty-two. Four years ago she came to our church, explaining that one reason she had chosen it was for help in raising her daughter. She knew that she didn't have long to live. At about the same time she learned she was pregnant, she was diagnosed with breast cancer. She had tried for so long to have a child that her choice was clear. All the hormones surging through her body to give the baby life meant that the cancer would grow fast; chemotherapy was ruled out by the pregnancy. What a terrible choice — between treating the cancer and having the child. Her little girl is three now.

"So we danced Job. I told my students the story and asked them simply to move the tragedy with me. Moving helps us know the sorrow in a way beyond words; words simply can't touch this reality. It's also a way to show that, despite it all, we're still trying to walk with God. The dance gives life by drawing people together. If people ever experience prayerful dance once — either by observing or participating — they know we're not necessarily having fun or being pretty. We're letting our souls move us.

"The dance also restores a conviction we've lost — that we are beautiful, gifted people worthy of care. Our ideas have merit and our bodies, in all shapes and forms, are creations of God. So many people feel adrift and wounded. When I teach dance I try to convey affirmation in different ways. Little by little, people absorb the message of blessedness."

A Healthy Distance from Church

"How does it relate to the church? The authority structure doesn't value women with gifts and brains. I got fired from a position as pastor because I asked too many questions. It made too many people uncomfortable when I wanted to unite the church with the neighborhood. The authorities prefer to stay within the church walls, talk to each other, preach safety, do it 'the church way.' I found very little that was Christ-like about it; it's healthier for me to stay away.

"So I sometimes advise others, 'Get out! Heal! Connect with people who have similar passions, hopes, and faith. Be the church in your own way, with people you can gather together. That is, after all, how it *began.*'

"I'm exploring alternative ministries now. Oh, they may not be labelled that, but I'm using the pastoral and organizational skills I learned in the seminary to embody the gospels in our neighborhood. These aren't ready-made jobs; people are creating their own. A little cluster of people say, 'We can do this!' and they find a way.

"Funny, I say I've left the church, but I really haven't. Maybe I've just moved to the margins, trying to bring what wholeness I can into the situations I find, and praying for the seeds I plant. I haven't given up my ordination and I don't want to. My denomination, like most, is anti-gay/lesbian. One of my friends was honest and told them she was lesbian; her standing was revoked. In other words, they reward secrecy, punish the outspoken truth!"

More Leverage Within?

"I have very little leverage staying in. But sometimes I wonder if it's even worth bothering to try to redeem the church. It's like trying to change an absolute monarchy. Sure, the church has changed gradually through the centuries, but it's also caused enormous pain in the process. For instance, I'm ordained, but I can't get a job. When I've interviewed, two churches have been honest enough to say, 'We're not ready for a woman pastor here.' But most are secretive, thus more insidious. The women who succeed in the system are usually conformists who don't do anything unusual.

"Decisions are made by a pulpit committee that represents a cross section of the congregation, men and women as well as different ages. So it's not an old boys' club, but attitudes are still ingrained. To them 'minister' means a man, preferably with a 'little wife and 2.3 kids.'

"Meanwhile, I'm learning that using 'the Reverend' before my name helps me slip into some other contexts. I'm working now with a group called 'Namaste,' from the Hindu meaning, 'the holy in me greets the holy in you.' We've put together a team of doctors, nurses, massage therapists, social workers, and I'm the chaplain. We have a couple of Jews, a couple of Catholics, a Hindu, and an agnostic. We do long-term care for people who have a terminal diagnosis or who are in chronic pain. We're just starting now, but we're already finding that outside the institution, people get pretty creative!

"I also want to start a neighborhood grassroots ministry to help women who want to make friends. Mother-to-Mother intentionally links low-income women with those whose incomes are adequate. We'll connect different cultural backgrounds and age groups in small clusters of two to four. It's ironic that to get started, we'll need a grant and a board — back to the trappings of the institution!"

Somehow, one suspects that it would be a long time before any institution in which Laura engaged would become calcified and rigid. To grassroots ministry as well as to liturgy, she brings the grace of the dance. She beautifies the margins.

– Part II –

Pivots and Pirouettes

"We're lost, but we're making good time!"
— YOGI BERRA

It's happened again. After another institutional decision that hurt people I respect and denied the justice the church claimed to preach, I was seething. Driving home, I gnashed teeth, pounded the steering wheel, went through the whole repertoire of angry gesture and word.

Then I saw the sign at the side of the road. Wobbly printing on cardboard proclaimed: "Pet Self Wash." In flooded the images: gerbils in showers, poodles soaping their curls, iguanas smoothing on fragrant lotions after a hot bath. Suddenly, anger dissolved in giggles. Perhaps on another day, the sign would have been merely quaint or interesting; because I was so tightly wired today, it became howlingly funny.

Not that the anger wasn't justified. Not that I won't return to the issues. But for a moment, it had simply become irrelevant — the sign a quick distraction from a cause that could become grim and self-righteous. Nothing can annoy us more than friendly (often, ironically sober) advice to "lighten up" when we're legitimately upset. But when some unexpected intervention turns aside our own wrath and brings us humor, that's a gift.

This section is about turnings more profound than a mood swing. It begins with a poem about Mary at perhaps the most stunning turning point in history: the annunciation. Another bib-

lical figure, Thomas, and two historical figures, Vincent van Gogh
and Mechthild of Magdeburg, also made major shifts in direction.
Three contemporary figures have done the same: finding the church
frustrating or irrelevant, they have found other places to work out
their gospel mandates. Moving beyond individuals to groups, we
look at a parish caught between their mission of compassion and
the intrusion of higher leadership. Summarizing the whole section
is a chapter on imagining a church larger than any boundaries that
have previously defined it.

Just as dance has direction and purpose, so does any meaningful
life. Many people find that conversion or a constant turning becomes a regular movement which prevents stagnation. So for those
described here, the momentum of life nudges them *from* one place
to another. May it encourage all who feel trapped or paralyzed to
make a bold step, a pivot, a pirouette.

After the Annunciation

The heartbreak of that sentence —
"And the angel left her."

So she knew it too:
the door's abrupt thud, the windowless room,
the stagnant air in the prison of appearances,
endless time unrolling from empty spool.

She must have learned to strain on tiptoe,
to yearn beyond imagining, keenly attuned
to each shadow, pulse, sudden twilight hush
in case the angel came again.

She would recognize the hints: a glimmer
underlining the door, a tremor in her hand,
the voice like a flute spiraling in silence,
the air stirred and sparkled by wing.

5

From Question to Invitation

T H O M A S

Thomas gets a bad rap. To him we almost automatically attach the surname "Doubter," when it is more appropriate to honor Thomas as a seeker. The other name given him in John 20:24 is the Twin — and we may often feel like Thomas's twin in spirit. The Greek name Didymus comes from the same root as "divided," and Thomas Didymus could stand as patron saint for those who undergo the particular torture of the divided self. He is called "one of the twelve" yet was absent from Jesus' first postresurrection appearance to the company. Perhaps his untimely absence symbolizes an attitude with which we can sometimes identify: his not-quite-total participation, his hanging back on the fringe of the crowd. "Wait just a minute!" he protests when the disciples breathlessly announce, "We have seen the Lord!" The memory of wounds and nail marks are still fresh in his mind; he will not be rushed into compliance just to be "one of the guys."

The same feeling may cross our minds as a full church joins in exuberant song, or as friends glom enthusiastically onto the newest book, speaker, or theory. Part of us may long to be "one of the twelve," secure in the community of faith; part hesitates, questions, resists jumping on another bandwagon. We have been hurt before; we have learned to protect ourselves in a sensitive area, as one favors an ankle that has been broken, long after the original injury. People who do not understand this predicament are quick to label us cynics or skeptics; they have not peered into that dark corner of the soul that craves companionship, that longs fiercely to fall easily in line with all the others and not be branded "doubter." The child's desire to look like everyone else, to not wear the odd clothes or the wrong shoes, still tempts those who cower behind a confident adult appearance.

What's admirable about Thomas is his willingness to voice the questions that knot his stomach and clog his throat. Too many of us suppress those misgivings because we've been trained to be polite or agreeable, or we've been socialized by a clerical or churchy culture. "That teaching ignores people's lived experience, or flies in the face of the gospel," we murmur to ourselves. We tell our closest friends our suspicions that the church acts unjustly — then swear them to secrecy. What we might recognize as crime in any other setting, we forgive when it's done on church property. If a filmmaker or an artist were silenced or suppressed the way theologians are, we'd invoke the principles of free speech or academic freedom. We like our blinders, and we like them snug. In the face of the other disciples' conviction, we might swallow a natural skepticism and nod gladly in agreement, just to be part of the crowd.

But Thomas blurts it out. If for no other reason, we might honor him for his honesty, his willingness to risk and be wrong. He puts it baldly, a characteristic we have come to admire in church members who aren't afraid to "speak the truth to power." Just as no one can fire a person who has retired, no one can slander a person whose convictions are clear.

Jesus' Response to Thomas

It's fascinating to observe how Jesus treats Thomas in return. The disciple's questioning is not met with ridicule, but with invitation. Jesus' words imply the stage directions: he must have not only told Thomas "give me your hand"; he must have reached for it. He must have not only said, "Put it into my side"; he must have gently guided it there.

Jesus asks Thomas to draw closer, to touch more intimately, to enter his wounds more directly and bond more tightly than any of the others. In their unquestioned peace, which some might term blissful ignorance, the other disciples stand further from the Christ who places Thomas's hand into the nail marks, into the wounded side. That exploration of the Risen Lord's body horrifies us at one level, but at another we envy such intimacy. Thomas reaches into the depths of Jesus' body and finds the contours familiar.

That hollow beneath the ribs might symbolize the empty place in himself, tortured by his own skepticism, longing for certainty. It is a space Jesus knows well. "In the Easter appearances this man Christ stood, as it were, in that 'place' in the disciples where God alone can come and go. This particular person, totally human and totally God, gives himself to be experienced in that place of ultimate emptiness and longing which is our transcendence, our creatureliness, where only God...can be present."[25]

Perhaps Christ found in Thomas's anguish the echo of his own tortured prayer in the garden. Perhaps he welcomed Thomas onto common ground: in the shadowy doubt, not the firm certainty, Thomas is twinned with Jesus. Furthermore, Christ extends the bond between them to include all those not yet born, who had not seen with clarity but would follow the same shaky, uncertain pathway Thomas forged.

Looking down the centuries, Jesus saw us: our qualms and frustrations, our anger and bitterness. "You believe because you can see me," he told our twin. "Happy are those who have not seen and yet believe." His words reach down the corridor of time and wrap us in reassurance. Those who don't rush in with all flags flying; those who entertain serious doubt; those too hurt or drained to summon robust belief; those who resist uncritical acclaim: Jesus calls them blessed too.

Jesus' response is notable for its lack of coercion. In his voice we hear no trace of "you *will* believe this" or "you won't even *think* about that." In his delicate touch we feel none of the strong-arm tactics with which churchgoers have become uncomfortably familiar. Such forced submission of will and intellect, such threats to those who question, do violence to the freedom and creativity of some of the church's finest thinkers.

The Contemporary Question

While examples abound, one from the Catholic tradition will suffice here. Father Bernard Häring's writings on sexual and medical ethics were challenged by the Vatican's Congregation for the Doctrine of the Faith. They examined him from 1975 to 1979, as he suffered from throat cancer. The struggle began over his protest against *Humanae vitae,* the papal document on birth control. Though known for his gentleness, Häring sharply criticized church authorities after his trial.

He wrote the prefect of the Congregation for the Doctrine of the Faith:

> During the Second World War I stood before a military court four times. Twice it was a case of life and death. At that time I felt honored because I was accused by enemies of God. The accusations then were to a very large extent true, because I was not submissive to that regime. Now I am accused by the Doctrinal Congregation in an extremely humiliating manner. The accusations are untrue. In addition, they come from a very high organ of the church leadership, an organ of that church which I in a long life have served with all my power and honestly hope to serve still further with sacrifice. I would rather stand once again before a court of war of Hitler.[26]

Ironically, the same Häring who disagreed so publicly and argued so eloquently with Pope Paul VI's position was asked to give the annual retreat for the same pope and the curia.[27] Such paradoxes would probably not seem unusual to Thomas. In the best of all worlds, the world of the resurrected Lord and the enlightened church, questioners are not shameful gatecrashers, but honored guests. Indeed, the novelist Graham Greene believed that a less certain church would be a more humane one. He once asked, "Isn't it lack of doubt that gives rise to fanaticism?"

The risen Christ welcomes longing in whatever shape it may take, and meets it with his own burning desire for the individual. He gives Thomas exactly what he needs, in exactly the terms Thomas expresses it. Remaining true to character, he offers us no less.

Your turn:

- What parallels do you find between Thomas's experience and your own?

6

From Clergy to Art

VINCENT VAN GOGH

Thank you, Reverend Mr. deJong. Your name may be unknown, but you did humanity a great service. You told Vincent van Gogh that he could not study to be a minister.

Few people know how ardently the young van Gogh longed to evangelize, to be a minister like his father. Paternal expectations exerted a steady pressure: as Vincent wrote to his brother Theo about their father, "His heart is burning within him that something may happen to enable me to follow him in his profession; Father always expected it from me."[28]

That weight was matched by the intensity of Vincent's own desire. It was such a simple thing: van Gogh wanted only to preach in some little country church, to minister to the miners whom he described as haunted by their "longing for the 'old, old, story.' "[29] The lives of these people, who seemed always covered by coal dust, were miserable, grimy, disease-ridden, desperately poor. All Vincent wanted was to bring them the joy of the gospel. Yet he could not afford a seminary education and seemed ill-suited for it.

He studied intensely for exams, but even as he records his struggles with algebra and Greek, his descriptions of landscapes are full of vitality. He admits the irony: "I sometimes have had a lesson from a hay-mower that was of more use to me than one in Greek."[30] He is sensitive to details and colorations in nature that few people ever see. The work of other painters like Rembrandt or Millet brings him a joy missing from the descriptions of his studies. "How rich art is! If one can only remember what one has seen, one is never idle or truly lonely, never alone."[31]

He criticized the church institution in the same scathing terms he used for the art establishment. Both, it seemed, rejected the creative in favor of the tried and true. While he wrote in 1878, his condemnation carries surprisingly modern overtones:

> I must tell you that it is with evangelists as with artists. There is an old academic school, often detestable, tyrannical, the accumulation of horrors, men who wear a cuirass, a steel armor of prejudices and conventions; those people when they are at the head of affairs, dispose of positions, and by a rotary system they try to keep their protégés in their places, and to exclude the other man.[32]

Always desperate for money, disappointed in his hopes for evangelizing, frustrated in his desire to share the lot of the miners, van Gogh languished for some years while Theo worried that he was not productive. Yet the turning point came when van Gogh wrote with Easter overtones: "In spite of everything I shall rise again; I will take up my pencil, which I have forsaken in my great discouragement, and I will go on with my drawing; and from that moment everything seemed transformed for me."[33] He probably scratched out these words from a cold garret in bad light, but the moment calls for an Alleluia chorus, a thunder of applause, confetti, and the gratitude of thousands.

Not that the epiphany led to instant fame: van Gogh sold only one painting in his lifetime and was constantly rejected and scorned. Part of the problem may have been his difficult personality; he alienated everyone but his brother, an art dealer who tried to help by supplying paints and canvas. In turn, Vincent poured out his heart in letters to Theo, the only one he did not alienate with his abrasiveness. Sensitive in all things, van Gogh was not blind to his own temperamental problems and described his personality in terms of a poignant scene he might have sketched: "There may be a great fire in our soul, and no one ever comes to warm himself at it; the passers-by see only a little bit of smoke coming through the chimney, and pass on their way."[34]

What if van Gogh had continued the career in the church which he so longed for in his twenties? Then we might not have had the vases of sunflowers which sing off the page, the flaming fields of golden hay, the pulsing, starry sky, the country road caught up in the swirl of cypresses, grasses and clouds overhead, the lines that lasso the wind, the throbbing dynamism of hills and rooftops we assumed were stationary. Van Gogh had an eye for beauty in the commonplace, a sensitivity to bark, twig, marsh, and elderly miner that led many people after his death to "warm themselves at his hearth."

Like any extremely sensitive person, van Gogh had serious internal conflicts. After a quarrel with Gauguin, he mutilated his ear, then looked at himself in the mirror and painted a self-portrait. He died from a self-inflicted wound to the stomach. Though van Gogh's struggles were perennial and his personality problems remained constant, his happiness in his art recurs as a theme throughout his life. Perhaps this note sounds even stronger because any public acclaim he received was posthumous. What fed his feverish output was not sales, applause, or awards, but an inner flame. He would probably have brought a similar enthusiasm to the ministry, but the world is richer because he changed his course.

Indeed, van Gogh achieved a unique blend of art and theology which enriched humanity. He expressed his goal: "In a picture, I want to say something comforting, as music is comforting. I want to paint men and women with that something of the eternal truth which the halo used to symbolize."[35]

Today, people still agonize over a rejection from a particular type of ministry. Might a change of direction be for them as fruitful as it was for van Gogh? They may not be brilliant artists or come anywhere close to his talent. But a gesture like his picking up the pencil might nurture their inner happiness. For them, the clanging shut of the church door might create a new niche. The story of van Gogh gives substance to the truism about God's shutting a door and opening a window.

Your turn:

- Van Gogh's "resurrection" after being denied a ministry came from picking up a pencil. If you have had frustrations like his, imagine yourself making a similar gesture. What, for you, corresponds to the lifting of the pencil? How do you feel when you channel your energies in the direction of that creative outlet?

- How does van Gogh's experience with the church echo or parallel yours?

For Mechthild on Her Feast

A day of faxes and frequent flier miles
E-mails and answering machines
conference calls, strategic planning.
All terms that would bewilder her:

Except the high wild wing of desire
beating fast against the cage, trying
not to squander self on anything less
than the heart's deepest urge.

Except the self, ennobled and adorned
by lover's image, immersed in God as
fish in sea or bird riding sleeve of air
reaching always toward the unmingled wine.

Except the thirst, made beautiful by object,
responding to God's tender call: "O thou!"
As the deer delicately arcs one foot,
places one hoof in the onrushing stream.

7

From Exile to Torrent of Love

MECHTHILD OF MAGDEBURG

Imagine having tea with Mechthild of Magdeburg. Bend to enter a room which is small but cozy, simple but comfortable. The warm tones of wood on the carved chairs, ceiling, and walls glow in the firelight. The day is drizzly; the first cool of autumn is in the air, so pull your armchair closer to the hearth. Mechthild enters, carrying a plump tea pot and rolls still warm from the oven. Like many German homes, hers is full of kitchen aromas.

You relax in your chair, feeling at ease, yet knowing that hunger for more than food brings you here. You have traveled across time because you suspect that Mechthild can nurture you at some deep level, some place within that is lost and alone. She is known not only for her homely skills, but as God's *hausfrau*. She imagined her relationship with God in terms familiar, yet mysteriously transformed: "Thy childhood was a companion of My Holy Spirit; thy youth was a bride of My humanity, in thine old age thou art a humble housewife of My Godhead."[36]

You have chosen Mechthild as a mentor because she is a soulmate who struggled with the church and survived. Your own struggles will not seem foreign to her. She was brutally honest about her own battles with church hierarchy. Her criticism was anything but veiled or polite: "God calls the cathedral clergy goats because their flesh stinks of impurity with regard to eternal truth."[37] She compared the church to one whose skin is filthy, unclean. Needless to say, her vivid attacks did not win her gold stars with the clergy. Instead, her criticisms led to charges of heresy, refusal of holy communion, exile, and repudiation.

As a coping strategy, though she would never call it that, Mechthild did an interesting, internal pivot that the rest of us could model. She turned from the institutional arena, which was not life-giving, to the contemplation of God's very nature, so life-giving she referred to it frequently as a torrent of love. To people whose images of God were narrow and punitive, she introduced God as passionate lover, who longs for mysterious intimacy with the soul. When the barriers between human and divine constituted far heavier blockades than they do today, she proposed a relationship with God that was as natural as a fish in water or a bird in air.

Near the end of her life, she wondered why she was still alive. Only after her death could that doubt be answered. In her sixties, Mechthild inspired other women to write, an action which in their day was brazen, unheard of. Mechthild broke the silence, and soon after her books appeared the writings of two women who lived in her same convent, Gertrude the Great and Mechthild of Hackeborn. Scholars think that the younger visionaries were inspired by Mechthild.[38]

But enough of biography. Warmed by the tea and the fire, the conversation begins. Mechthild might speak in imagery:

"I see myself immersed in the flowing of a 'minne-flut,' the torrent of love which does many things. It brings together various streams, all the fragments of our lives, and at the same time cleanses or sloughs off what is inconsequential. That vast flow carries sticks and leaves, berries and pebbles on the surface churning. But go deeper and find the still pools, the clear, transparent spaces where the light is contained."

Mechthild's model exemplifies the truth discovered by many seekers: to get past the surface turmoil, meditate more. Go deeper. Which Mechthild apparently did. Despite her ongoing struggle with religious leaders of her time, what predominates in her writing is not bitterness but joy. The clergy may have been goats, but God was lover. Her poetry in the courtly love tradition makes the soul the object of God's desire:

> O thou! image of My Divine Godhead,
> Ennobled by My humanity,
> Adorned by My Holy Spirit.... [39]

We are used to praising God, to honoring the Trinity, to singing hymns about the divine. But to reverse the dynamic, to have God seeking and flattering *me*, seeing in *me* God's reflection — well, that is a new twist. In short, we are used to addressing God as "thou," but surprised when God returns the favor and honors us.

We can respond to God as Mechthild did, with clear assurance. We too can reach the point of the psalm where we can agree: "My body is completely at rest." Contemporary images might express that state like this:

> I am hammock-rocked.
> I am sun-dappled.
> I am peak achieved.
> I am tight embrace.
> I am easy laughter.
> I am kite in high wind.
> I am lantern kindled.
> I am prow slicing white wave.
> I am pod bursting with seed.
>
> I know who I am.

Your turn:

- As you imagined yourself having tea with Mechthild, what did she say to ease your hurt from the church, your struggle with the church, your frustration with the church?

- Add your own image to the list directly above. Complete this sentence: When I am strong and sure in myself and centered in God, I feel like....

8

From Parish Council to Prison Ministry

MAURA

Maura's dark eyes flash with enthusiasm as she refills plates and plunges into dinner conversation. A member of a Catholic religious community, she has moved past her order's stricter traditions, yet remains faithful to its core value of service. Over the years that commitment has taken many forms, from teaching first grade to directing children's retreats to working as a parish director of religious education. Now she works for Empowerment, an agency that helps women who are in jail or have been in jail to get off drugs, earn their GED certificates, reshape their lives. It is both the most heartbreaking and the most exhilarating work she has ever done.

"There I was," she laughs. "Brandishing my master's degree in scripture at God. I had worked hard to get it, but none of the jobs that might use my training were materializing. I thought I'd be teaching the Bible; instead I'm going to the weekly meetings of the prostitute support group!

"The first time I heard their stories, I had to keep one hand over my mouth, to keep my jaw from dropping open. Some of the women were forced into prostitution by their parents or husbands. One was thrown out of the house at fifteen. Fifteen! My mother wouldn't even let me babysit at fifteen!

"And yet, after a lifetime of work in parishes and parochial schools, I heard more support from the prostitutes around that table than I'd ever felt at a church committee meeting. After each one spoke of her struggles to go straight, the others would shout their encouragement: 'You go girl! You ditch that pimp! You don't have to take that stuff!' The pep talks were accompanied by practical help: 'You can stay at my house.' 'I got a place.'

"I can't imagine what kind of places they are," Maura rolls her eyes. "But no matter how little they have, they're willing to share it.

"The first time I visited the jail, I had to get security clearance. 'Uh oh,' I said to the officer. 'Do speeding tickets count?'

" 'Sister,' he answered. 'You're gonna see far worse things in here.' The first woman I met was tiny, maybe ninety pounds. After taking years of abuse herself, she saw her husband start in on their child. She slit him with the kitchen knife all the way up the middle. Another woman was the 'fourth most wanted' on the post office list. She wanted to know 'Who are the top three? How can I get ahead?' This same woman bemoaned the fact that nuns no longer wear habits, so you can't hear them coming — no warning click of rosary beads!

"A woman in jail for drug possession once gave me her definition of God. 'God is Toby, Jamie, and my girls. Toby is my friend who won't sell me crack when I'm trying to stay off it. Jamie is the truck driver who lets me sleep in the cab of his truck when I'm homeless — and doesn't even ask for sex, or any payment in return.' And her girls? Her own mother abandoned her, so she didn't have much of a role model. She says of her failures with her children, 'The one thing I wanted to be in life was a mother, and I can't do that.' "

Maura comments: "In all the years I studied theology, I never saw a definition of God as a crack dealer, a truck driver, or three little girls in foster care. It's kind of incarnational, isn't it?"

In one of the little dramas that compose her day, Maura makes a quick run to the hospital. One of "her girls" has delivered her baby. She comments as she drives: "It was touching how she tried to stay off coke during her pregnancy so the baby wouldn't be born addicted. She's already lost two children to social services and is determined to keep this one. But how pathetic — I only met her a few months ago. I'm pretty much a stranger, yet I'm the one she calls when the baby's born. She needs help spelling her daughter's name for the birth certificate!"

Asked about the institutional church, a wave of sadness sweeps over Maura. All the energy drains away; her face looks older than usual. "Ah, it's so sad how they've ruined it. All our dreams and expectations gone. One of my friends, another sister, was doing wonderful ministry with the elderly. The parish priest called her on the carpet. Guess why? She'd been taking communion to the sick. He was concerned that her pyx (the vessel for carrying the consecrated bread) didn't have a velvet lining. She quit on the spot.

"It's hard to move from the world I'm in now, of drugs, prostitution, homelessness, and foster care, to one where somebody actually cares about a velvet lining! Could they get any further from reality?"

As quickly as possible, Maura changes the topic. When she returns to street-smart stories, the animation returns to her face. "I'll take your daughter to jail!" she promises, as nuns would have once held out the bribe of a holy card, a picnic at the motherhouse, or a snack after the prayer service. For Maura, the city streets and the jail contain more life than the church.

"When they open a window in our meeting room at the jail, all the incarcerated women rush to the open window for fresh air. It's usually so stuffy that they jostle each other for a chance to fill their lungs with oxygen. Do you think there might be a symbol here for the rest of us? We aren't in jail, but we're dragged down by invisible chains. Where's the fresh air for us?"

9

From Towering to Tiny

B E L L E

Belle is a quilter. From insignificant scraps and small patches, she creates beauty and pattern, overlapping color and intricate design. Her view of the church could fit right into a quilting frame. Her contribution there may seem small, but has been steady. She serves regularly on the welcoming team; she befriends many struggling people; she brings a casserole to a grieving family; she buys the punch and cookies for a reception. They are traditional, nurturing actions, and they cannot be underestimated. Without them, says the Book of Sirach, "no city can be inhabited" (38:32). It describes such people:

> . . . they are not found among the rulers.
> But they maintain the fabric of the world,
> and their concern is for the exercise of their trade. (38:34)

Asked about her own struggles, Belle replies, "Oh, I can't leave the church now. We all just do our one little piece at a time." It's an appropriate response from one who knows how valuable one small patch can be, how it takes its place in the overall design, how the wrong color or shape harms the whole. Belle's delicate fingers have arranged the tiny pieces of countless quilts; comparing her role in the church to patchwork neither demeans nor exaggerates her service.

Some will scoff, insisting that the demands of the age and the severity of the abuses call for radical overhaul. While their concerns are legitimate, something must be said for Belle and those like her, who care for one small segment, bring it all their energy, and do great good there. Such people capture some of Jesus' spirit because they tap the power inherent in smallness.

After all, he worked closely with twelve people — not twelve thousand. He was not impressed by mega-churches and stayed away from the professional religious types. He cured a handful of people, not everyone with an ailment. He revived a little girl, a widow's son, and a friend named Lazarus. But the power of his resurrection has convinced millions of people that death is not final and that life goes on forever.

While Belle has a name and a face, she has another whole co-hort of colleagues, whose names and faces are unknown. They live on roads like Lincoln Street, a busy thoroughfare that car-ries traffic through a Midwestern city. The homes along this street aren't palatial; many are duplexes or small, aging residences. Per-haps, as in many other arenas, the genius is in the detail. If the cars were to slow and observe, the drivers might notice the little treasures of Lincoln Street. One yard, for instance, blazes with a flower display that makes the City Botanic Gardens pale. An elderly, bent woman tends this riot of dahlias and daisies, corn-flowers and asters, roses and pansies. She probably does it for love of flowers, never dreaming how her garden brightens the day for all who pass it.

How fortunate to have, along such a popular route, the oasis Alice Walker describes in her book *In Search of Our Mothers' Gardens*. She speaks eloquently of women "abused and mutilated in body, dimmed and confused by pain," "crazy, loony, pitiful."[40] They were driven to madness because their creativity had no out-let; their lives consisted of slavery, child-bearing, and menial work. Any imaginative spark that was not stifled, they handed on to their children, like a sealed letter they could not read.

In this way, Walker's mother poured her artistry into her garden. Walker's memories of poverty are filtered by a screen of flowers because of her mother's creativity. The brilliance of color and the profusion of blooms drew strangers to the garden. But perhaps most important is its influence on the gardener herself: "I notice that it is only when my mother is working in her flowers that she is radiant, almost to the point of being invisible — except as Creator: hand and eye. She is involved in work her soul must have. Ordering the universe in the image of her personal conception of Beauty."[41]

All *that* going on, and passers-by think merely (if they notice at all), "what a lovely garden!" The same unguessed levels of meaning might be true for kindred spirits along the street. They keep their lawns mowed like jade carpets, hang wind chimes and seasonal banners, wish each other a pleasant "good evening." They are not wealthy people; they probably agonize over car repairs and doctor bills. The latest cultural trends, political squabbles, or scientific innovations mean little to those who wait for the bus along Lincoln Street. Yet their small courtesies grace the day, beautify the ordinary.

Outside the confines of the church can be found great goodness — when we tire of the politics, the wrangling, the power plays, it may be wise to look beyond church walls. A whole middle ground of folks don't get caught up in the squabbles and remain holy, happy people. They would ascribe to the theory that "You are not a saint because you keep the rules and are blameless; you are a saint if you live in the real world, going out and loving the real people whom God has put into your life."[42] A parallel might be found in the people of Jesus' time. At one end of the spectrum, the religious establishment was caught up in arguments over the afterlife, the law, the rules about curing on the Sabbath.

At the other end of the spectrum, a shepherd watched a flock, a mother mourned her dead son, a father worried about his sick daughter, a woman cooked a meal, a man collected taxes. Fairly mundane occupations, we'd say: yet they became part of Jesus' incarnation lived out, the essential substance of his healing ministry. Throngs of people responded to images they could understand, drawn not from esoteric theology but from daily life: leaven in bread dough, hay stored in barns, lamps on stands, weeds in a field, vines and branches. Today we still find it difficult to understand theory which has grown too abstract, which has lost its moorings in skin and bone.

Have we lost the knack of looking for holiness where Jesus did, among fisherfolk and cooks, soldiers and children? How can we extend our search for meaning beyond what's defined as holy or what the religious ghetto contains?

10

From "Do-Gooder" to Building Manager

J E A N

It began simply enough — coffee with Jean, a chance to catch up. She had, it developed, started from scratch to build affordable housing for the people of her town. Now she had eighty units occupied and forty more under construction. "Come see!" she pleaded. "It's not far."

Jean not only built housing that was affordable; she built solid, light-filled structures that won architectural awards. Ironically, a woman who hadn't known a pliers from a screwdriver was supervising professional carpenters and electricians. Proudly she showed off the laundry room, meeting room and children's play room for the residents. Children who'd described their previous living conditions as "dumps" now had homes where they weren't embarrassed to bring their friends.

Readily Jean admitted, "I was a fool for ever starting this." She probably downplayed the tough parts: the incredulous loan officers, the shrewd building permit supervisors, the skeptical funding agencies, even the residents who took advantage of her generosity. But she summed up the negatives of the experience, laughing: "I got over any naive do-gooderism fast!"

The full implications of Jean's work cannot be understood in isolation but take on richness when set in the context of a larger story: the account of the annunciation. The angel Gabriel is full of high-sounding promises, proclaiming phrases like "endless reign," "Son of the Most High," and "throne of David." Mary's response cuts to the chase: How can she have a child when she hasn't had sex? The angel's reassurance speaks to all people: "Nothing is impossible with God."

How the echoes of that line could radiate through Jean's life! Eight years before, anyone would have scoffed at the idea of one woman single-handedly tackling a town's massive housing problem. Now she had a paid staff of five, countless volunteers, and a flourishing program housing eighty families.

While Jean's example is dramatic, others can surely fit their own stories into the general lines of "nothing impossible." The boy with a serious learning disability who finished college and is now a brilliant teacher himself.... The woman who married late in life, thought she'd never have children, and is now the mother of three.... The girl who started out as the receptionist and is now the senior partner of the firm.... Countless, anonymous people, when they think about it, find it hard to believe how much they've accomplished in their chosen spheres.

While remaining faithful to her religious tradition, Jean didn't waste a minute discussing the failures of institutions or the sins of leaders. She was too busy getting on with her life. Why waste time fretting when she had plumbing to inspect, playgrounds to plan, and clients to interview? If someone else was stalled, why let it slow her down? An unclouded gospel imperative still called her forth.

Jean may not have known it, but she was practicing an attitude toward her religion which some call "holy indifference." In other words, when the institution fails, insults, or demeans its people, the healthiest response may be to ignore it. Why waste precious energies on what is hopelessly calcified? Nurture the alternatives!

Different people have different ideas about an approach which clearly works for Jean. Some may prefer to work patiently within the system for its reform. Power to them! But now and then, it's revitalizing to take a break. It's energizing to have coffee with Jean.

Your turn:

- Do you know a Maura, a Belle, a Jean, or someone like them? What qualities make these people so refreshing to be around?

- In what area of your life do you most see the truth of the saying, "Nothing is impossible with God"?

- Where do you stand along the spectrum of "holy indifference" to religious institutions? Are you more indifferent, more committed, or somewhere in between?

11

From Law to Compassion

PARABLE OF A PARISH

It was a fairly typical parish, with equal shares of busy-bodies and saints, the bewildered and the clear-eyed, the married-with-kids and never-married, the overweight and underweight, those who shared money and those who gave time. When they sang about "the young and the old, the frightened, the bold, the greatest and the least," they sang with special gusto, perhaps recognizing themselves in the lines of the hymn. Busy about many things, the people tended to gravitate toward their church on Sunday mornings, then give their talents to the larger world the rest of the week. They may have been out of touch with church politics, but they recognized crying need when they saw it.

As they did the day the mother of two young children died in a car accident. The pastor was out of town, but the people held an impromptu prayer service. The choir sang, the woman's brother read her favorite scripture, the pastoral associate gave a reflection, and all the people prayed especially hard for the family in mourning. The people also pitched in with more tangible help. They delivered dinners; they braided little girls' hair; they did laundry; they cleaned house. Volunteers cooked and served food after the funeral. They sent checks to help with funeral expenses and the children's education.

But the bishop called the pastor on the carpet, saying, "Why do you stand during the eucharistic prayer? Buy kneelers! Tell the people to kneel." His head down, the pastor returned to the people and told them that apparently the important thing, the sure-fire route to God, and the loftiest of values was a kneeling posture during the eucharistic prayer....

When homelessness became rampant in their city, the people

of the parish realized that their unused convent could house several families. The confirmation candidates painted the building, the preschoolers made welcome signs, the day care center collected soap and towels, the Heritage Club baked, the singles' group volunteered to take overnight shifts. The parish became part of a larger coalition with churches of many traditions.

Thus, seven homeless families became the guests of the Presbyterians one week, the Lutherans the next, this parish with its remodeled convent the following week. The logistics got complex, and the rotation had a few glitches, but the beds were comfortable and the food was abundant. The families had warm, safe places to stay. For a little while, they came in out of the cold. They took hot baths, ate voraciously, hugged their children with more zest. The people of the parish joined them for dinner on Friday night and they all worshiped together on Sunday morning. The liturgy took on new meaning for those who had experienced both the hospitality and vulnerability of Christ.

But the diocesan worship director called the pastor on the carpet saying, "We have heard worrisome rumors that you use whole wheat bread in your eucharistic services. Does it contain unsanctioned honey? Why do you not use the official wafers?" The pastor could not look into his people's eyes, so he stared at the floor as he told them that once again they had failed. Apparently the important thing, the glorious path to heaven, the guarantee of eternal salvation was to break official bread....

Now a child in the parish became very sick. At the age of three, he was diagnosed with leukemia. His hair fell out from chemotherapy; his skin turned a pasty white. So the people of the parish gathered for an anointing. Their pastor announced it quietly, after Mass one Sunday, and lots of people stayed. Old people with canes, parents with young children, single people, tired people, busy people. Most didn't know the young parents or the child, but they prayed in a powerful silence, extending their hands over the family. Then the pastor poured oils over the little boy, in a long tradition of anointing Christians for over two thousand years. The people prayed that he and his parents might have strength for whatever lay ahead, that they might be as Christ was: priest, prophet, and king. Those who were closest in the circle of support touched the mother, who held the boy in an embrace that reminded people of the Pietà. With tears in their eyes, they ended by singing "This Child of Yours," the song they always sang for baptisms.

Then the vicar of priests called the pastor on the carpet, saying, "We have heard from our informants that some of your lectors change the word 'men' to 'people.' They sometimes replace 'he' with 'them.' Do you not know the evils of inclusive language? Control these people! Stop them! If need be, silence the proclamation of the Word."

With shoulders slumping, the pastor returned to his parish. This time he could barely speak, but he whispered to the people. "Call everyone 'men.' Call your daughters 'sons,' your mothers 'fathers' and your aunts 'uncles.' Ignore everything you have learned from the age of two about language, and forget welcoming while you're at it. People who live in Italy will teach us English. Apparently the way to understand the mystery of God in our midst, the way to minister to those who ache with hurt, the way to attain holiness, is to use the male pronoun at all times."

Somewhat bewildered, the people tried to comply. But as they left the church that day, one particularly feisty member of the youth group was overheard asking, "Which of these, do you think, was a neighbor to the one who fell into the hands of the robber?"

12

From Narrow to Broader Church

God made so many different kinds of people, why would
[God] allow only one way to serve [God]?
— MARTIN BUBER

Kendra had seen much good work wiped out, many hours
wasted, when her labors for an international church organization were reviewed by the church officials. Useful
activities and thought-provoking resources were all rejected at one
stroke of the censor's pen. Her recourse?

"I whisper it to myself, sometimes between clenched teeth:
broader church. Broader church. I remember the time I spent in
Africa, with bishops who are pastoral, people who are enthusiastic.
I vow to return there at least twice a year — not only to encourage
them, but to renew my droopy spirits. And it works!"

St. Augustine said, "There are many who are of the church who
are not of God, and many who are of God who are not of the
church." When people struggle with their churches it's often because of an unjust policy or a leadership that's lost touch with
reality. Both Kendra and St. Augustine point beyond those battle
zones to a larger vision, the church as the people of God.

When we use the word "church" in this sense, introduced to
Catholics by the Second Vatican Council, it is easier to view it
more compassionately. We see then a whole assortment of folks:
the holy, the bumbling, the steadfast, the impulsive, the greedy, the
self-sacrificing, the eloquent, the inarticulate, the stodgy, the creative. Perhaps it is easier to view this "broader church" through
specifics: mini-portraits of people today.

Examples come from every sphere. A store owner, in complex
legal negotiations over the selling of her business, signs non-
compete clauses that severely restrict her ability to earn an income

for a period of two years. "Why did you do that?" her friends ask in astonishment. "It was the only way I could guarantee that my employees would still have jobs. Sure it's unfair. Sure it's corporate cruelty. But some of them have worked for me for twenty years. I had to protect them." In corporate politics, a grain of wheat still falls to the ground, someone still lays down a life for a friend.

Broader church. A blind woman comes to classes at a community center so she can get a better job. The tutor is already overwhelmed with people she needs to help: how will she work with the woman who is blind? No problem. Another woman who is terribly near-sighted offers to help, joking that it's a perfect chance for the blind to lead the blind. So the tutor writes large math problems on the blackboard. The near-sighted woman puts her nose a half inch away from the board, where she can squint to see. And the blind woman uses her little telescope. It's not a quick or efficient process, but it works. As little kids sing at Vacation Bible School, "Give God the glory, glory, children of the Lord."

A church big enough for all God's children. An elderly priest is a regular visitor at the county jail, where inmates keep secret his nickname: St. Valentine. Strict rules forbid correspondence between men and women in the building's two wings. But Valentine is willing to slip tiny papers into his pocket and carry notes back and forth. The guards don't suspect how innocent the messages are, laboriously printed, often looking like they were written by second graders: "How are you? I am fine. I love you." Sometimes a woman will ask him to make a phone call to her family: "Tell Bubba I love him." Or "Tell Mamacita to make sure the kids don't get into gangs." Dire warnings hang over his head: he could be subpoenaed if his little message service is ever intercepted. He ignores the threats, and God again is glorified.

An older, wiser church. Sometimes the people of God hint at why God fell in love with humanity. For an elderly Italian woman who has severe arthritis, getting out of bed and getting dressed is a painful, two-hour ordeal. When a visitor asks how she's doing she answers, "I keepa go. I keepa go." It may not be eloquent poetry. It may not be lofty theology. But it's not a bad motto for any who keep trying, who keepa go.

A younger church. The news from youth is encouraging. While some may argue that such optimism is unfounded, others are finding young spiritual seekers less confined than their parents were, open to the wisdom of many traditions, unburdened by anger. Young adults seem relatively untroubled by issues of power abuse and sexism in the church, looking to it instead for vibrant liturgies and social justice leadership.

They are suspicious of most institutions; after the Vietnam War, few, including the church, have earned their trust. A member of "Generation X" writes:

> Whether from the culture of cynicism in which we came of age, the irrelevance of church teaching to much of our daily life, the denigration of our experience in the formulation of that teaching or simply the overwhelming palette of religious options before us in the age of postmodernity, many in my generation have a spiritual identity that regards institutions with an underwhelmed dismissal: "Whatever."[43]

Commentator Tim Unsworth seconds this opinion: "They [youth] appear to have measurably less anger at the institutional church than many older Catholics, but this may be because they care measurably less."[44] Instead, they have focused their energies on care for the planet and the poor. In spiritual quests, they wrestle with ambiguity and seek the deeper meanings of popular culture. While youth have problems as did every generation, they can also be a source of hope, inspiring those grown jaded and depressed.

A church expanded by its martyrs. At a convention of liturgists, one tells the story of the catechist in Central America proclaiming the word to his base community. As he stood before the altar preaching, the gunmen entered and shot him down. So another catechist took his place and was also gunned down. And another, and another. The question posed to the professionals: "and what would liturgical guidelines say about blood on the altar?"

Meanwhile, the committees quibble over who should preach the word of God and what minor roles the laity can fill. Officials issue new directives, leaders write more letters, and the people yawn. The debates rage, but as always the little ones, the Hebrew *anawim,* or faithful remnant, give glory to God and broaden stuffy notions of what might constitute the church.

Your turn:

- How has your own concept of church been expanded past buildings, rules, and leaders?

– Part III –

Great Thirsts
and High Hopes

There is a river whose streams
make glad the city of God,
the holy habitation of the Most High.

—Ps. 46:4

Gathering at the [YMCA] Well

Nothing creates a stronger thirst than strenuous exercise, so we
cluster close to the water fountain, we members of Old Lady Aerobics Class. To an outsider, it would not be a pretty sight: the plump
bodies squashed into leotards as into sausage casings, the cellulite
and wrinkles and flab, the graying hair and sloping postures of the
middle-aged.

The fact that we show up regularly demonstrates either a
whacky humor or an impossible hope for fitness. We joke and
jostle in the rare freedom of those who have agreed to let each
other see our unguarded, blemished, imperfect selves. No make-
up or loose-fitting clothes camouflage our aging skin or thickening
waists. We come together like conspirators only for this class,
rarely see each other outside of it. Anonymity creates a strange
camaraderie.

We've replaced a hearty chorus of "Let's All Gather at the
River" with a gathering at the water fountain. There in the un-

likely setting of the YMCA gym bubbles our link to the ancient symbol. While the similarity doesn't spring to mind during aerobics, reflection afterward shows associations with baptism. There too the naked and vulnerable human has no camouflage for the flesh. There too life surges — the high hopes of friends and relatives like the support and healthy aspirations of people here. Most important, there as here and everywhere, the water symbolizes Christ's constant presence in our lives, making anywhere we go sacred ground.

This section considers how great desires relate to and inform our struggles. It begins with a poem describing a creative approach to oppression: if the authorities deny musical instruments, play the rivers! The biblical story shows Jesus calling forth the inner depths of the woman at the well. When she asks about the religious conflict between Samaritans, who worship on Mt. Gerizim, and Jewish people, who worship in Jerusalem, he dismisses both camps. "Don't look to either one," he tells her. "Look within. Inside of you a well bubbles up to eternal life."

His directive addresses our dilemmas as clearly today as it spoke to the Samaritan woman. Surrounded by the dry landscape of religious institutions, he sits by the well; he is the source of all that satisfies our thirst. Knowing that presence helps us modify our unrealistic expectations for the church. Plumbing the depths of our own wells, we have everything we need. As the poet June Jordan puts it: "we are the ones we have been waiting for."[45]

The stories that follow show how two women have followed Jesus' advice to forget the battles of religious adversaries and tap the springs of their inner wells. In keeping with the tone of cool blue wells, a meditation on nature's solace concludes this section.

Drumming the Rivers

Denied the musical instruments
reserved to men, Zaire women
play the rivers like drums,
beating tempos on the waters,
chanting rhythms slapped on waves.

Without score, without concert hall,
without formal black silk gown,
beneath feathery palm silhouettes
they ply the shining surface, an arc
of droplets flying from their hands.

Over loads of laundry, foam bubbling
on bare arms in the African morning,
they do not discuss oppression. Fluid,
spontaneous, they sing the liquid words
and drum the vibrant pulse of liberation.

13

Great Desires

What are your deepest desires? The question may seem irrelevant to those who struggle with more pressing issues. Asked this question, most people would hesitate, stumble, stall. As well they should. It doesn't prompt easy answers, and it moves the discussion from the immediate fray to another plane. Paradoxically, it helps us return to the pressing issue with clearer vision and deeper calm.

For if taken seriously, the question leads to a long and thoughtful process that unfolds over time. We are not talking here of the superficial desires most people could name quickly. Satisfying these needs fills most of our time: achieving job satisfaction, financial security, and mental stimulation; feeding and clothing ourselves and our loved ones; meeting our commitments. These are all good things, which consume much time and energy.

But there is something deeper, greater. Answering the question of desire may bring a shift in the lens through which we see our struggles — a shift that makes all the difference. Once we have identified our deep desires, everything else assumes a proper perspective. Note the word "identifying," not "achieving"; more on that later. The process of finding the deep desires creates a path into the soul. It leads us beyond what is pressing and good to what is great and abiding.

It would be tragic to leave the longings of our hearts unvoiced, unarticulated, brushed aside in deference to someone else, or for lack of time to explore them. God has planted in us profound longings that correspond to the largeness of God's self and God's dreams for us. To recognize this is to see ourselves as people "whose very being longs for God with a longing reflecting God's desire for the person."[46] Our problem often seems to be not that we desire too much, but that we desire too little. The creator of the universe yearns to bestow lavish abundance, but we skimp, confine, and restrain ourselves to what's sensible, manageable, prudent.

Yet the saints shake us out of our self-imposed restrictions, stunning us with even one glimpse of God. Catherine of Siena writes, "You have nothing infinite except your soul's love and desire."[47] It follows that desire is "the greatest source of human vitality and passion which God has given us."[48] Whenever we sincerely respond to a desire, we are responding to God's grace.

If God has given us talent and placed us on a large stage, how can we justify taking the bit parts or cowering behind the scenes? One of the most dramatic changes Jesus made was in his followers. Timid, fear-filled, prone to mistakes, they became lion-hearted saints under his influence. Wouldn't it be logical that he would have the same effect on us? Our struggles with church could be only part of a call to find a larger arena, invest our energies where they are appreciated, become less myopic, and enter greater happiness.

A Life-Long Search

A retreat setting, with empty stretches of time and space, is an ideal place to begin the search. The retreat house can also provide experienced guides. They serve like visitors to a foreign city who have been there before and know its configuration, or hikers on a path who know where the turns, best views, and steep slopes are. The guide will ask gently, "What are the greatest desires of your heart?" sometimes adding a person's name for emphasis. It seems innocent, but it begins a search that can last throughout a lifetime.

Even though the quest may be launched at a particular time with a particular guide, it soon takes on a life of its own. Different traditions may have different terminologies and emphases, but most would concur that an ongoing consideration of our deep desires is an integral part of any attempt to live reflectively.

So if we must be hounded by something heavenly, this question is more a faithful companion than a slobbering dog. We would miss it if it didn't surface regularly during times of prayer. If we are smart, we'll admit it's the *sine qua non;* without it we do not take ownership of our spirituality. If we have not meditated on this, we have not lived the examined life.

How freeing it is to know why we are on earth, to gain some inkling of the design God had for us at our creation. We can easily eliminate the side trips if we've established the main highway. Other topics and projects may furnish interesting subjects for debate, but they can be brushed aside if they have little to do with the deepest desires. Those goals become lodestones; they shine clear as the north star; from them, we set our compasses.

Sometimes people need to learn pathways into their own hearts to see what lies there. We are so accustomed to external stimulation and direction that we often place authority outside ourselves. That displacement may be one reason we become disillusioned with church authorities. Yet, "authority figures do not really validate personhood, goodness or personal authenticity. These realities exist prior to any affirmation."[49]

It might be easier to live by someone else's rules or dictates, but in the long run, that life has less integrity. It is far harder, and more significant, to find those unique guidelines that God has set within our hearts. They are personalized, after all, a sure map to bring us back to one who created us. Once we have named the desires, little else matters. We breathe the deep breath of D. H. Lawrence's poetic lines:

> All that matters is to be at one with the living God
> To be a creature in the house of the God of life.[50]

At home with God, at home with ourselves: what more could we ask?

Ah, but that goal was a preview. What still lies ahead is the hard work of discovering the desires. Preventing most of us from seeing our own best, truest self is a constant preoccupation with lesser things. Our busy-ness in itself isn't the problem; the problem comes when it controls our lives. Then we start losing our grasp on what's important. Sometimes the sense of who we are starts eroding. We become frantic and brusque, saying things we never intended because we don't take time to consider them. We act quickly and impulsively because we must rush to the next thing. The agenda determines all, and in the chaos we forget that we are more than our various functions.

In contrast, the great desires are yearnings so deep we sometimes can't articulate them. They are one of the most basic ways God speaks to us, but the dialogue doesn't come easily. Finding thoughtful responses requires a deliberate clearing of the surface. It's a persuasive argument for regular prayer.

So we settle in, hunker down, go through many layers of ourselves until we reach far below the surface. Most people must repeat the search regularly, going to the same quiet place over a period of time. Maybe it's the same rock by the river, the same "prayer chair," the same park. But authentic reflection seems to require revisiting and ample time.

Changes over Time

Impulses that change from month to month aren't the deepest desires. But change throughout a lifetime is expected. Someone in her early twenties, for instance, might long to establish a secure home, a solid relationship, a fulfilling career. By the time this person reaches her mid-thirties, many of those things are already set in place or under way. She now wants a different kind of intimacy. As children are born and grow, she lives through them, her deep desires wound about their well-being, their futures. As they leave, her desires shift again, perhaps in directions set aside when her energies poured into raising a family. Always the desires are embodied, colored by relationships and situations.

We can trust that in identifying and working toward them, we go with God. God, who created for us this unique plan, this particular dream, will not abandon us until it reaches fulfillment. On this point, we have the assurance of scripture both in word: "And God who has begun this good work in you will bring it to completion," and in image: "If the God we worship is imaged in a mother's love, how could we ever fear peril? How could our deepest heart's desires not be met? Even in the midst of threats or most painful relinquishments, we need not worry. The love that holds us close is the final act."[51]

Trusting in that kind of love helps us not only to survive struggle, but deepens our relationship with God. According to the mystics, desire is "the human being's most precious resource, and when we spend it heedlessly, we lose forever what it would otherwise purchase — nothing less than union with our own truest self."[52] Mechthild of Magdeburg imagined God saying:

> Thy heart's desire shalt thou lay nowhere
> But in mine own Divine Heart
> And on my human breast.
> There alone wilt thou find comfort
> And be embraced by My Spirit.[53]

This insight might explain her shift "from exile to torrent of love." Her vision was not the fruit of an agenda imposed from without, but sprang from inner desires.

Contemporary Examples: *Cold Mountain*

Jesuit priests have written much of the literature on desires, although each religious tradition has similar themes in different language.[54] The problem with many examples, however, is that they come from a clerical culture. While this may be helpful to the ordained, it is only indirectly helpful to the laity. Let's look instead at examples of lay people in popular culture, none of them especially "churchy," but all driven by great desire.

Charles Frazier's novel *Cold Mountain* has won the National Book Award, critical acclaim, and popular affection. It recounts the story of Inman, a Civil War soldier wounded in battle who leaves the front and journeys home. He is a sensitive man, wounded at a psychic level deeper than the scar on his neck. Horrible memories of war reverberate in his soul. His journey home is full of killing, hunger, brutality, betrayal, and, now and then, the unexpected kindness of strangers. As Inman's long, meandering walk continues, it becomes clear that it is driven by his memory of Ada.

A typical Charleston belle before the war, Ada must manage a home in an isolated area after the death of her father. Initially, she is unable even to feed herself, but as Inman walks, she undergoes a parallel progress. With the help of Ruby, she tackles chores probably unheard of for cultured women of their day, learning how to rake hay and slaughter chickens, plant and harvest, survive in a harsh environment. She becomes leaner, tougher, and more independent, though she still preserves that part of herself that sketches flowers and loves poetry.

Chapters alternate between Inman and Ada as the reader begins to grow more involved in their stories and to hope for their eventual reunion. He clings to the memory of her; an old letter is enough to carry him hundreds of miles. Overwhelmed by the changes in her life, she nevertheless writes him a line of encouragement. Theirs is the perfect example of a deeper desire underlying the pressing struggle for survival. When they are finally reunited, in the midst of a bitter blizzard, they glimpse something of what the other has endured. Inman touches the back of Ada's neck, a curve which he had admired during a party five years before. He describes the achievement of a deep desire: "There was a redemption of some kind, he believed, in such complete fulfillment of a desire so long deferred."[55]

They have several days together, expressing their love, describing their pasts, and feverishly planning their future together. Then Inman is killed, dying in Ada's arms. The reader may be saddened that they are denied a future, but looking at the tragedy from the standpoint of desire puts the story in a new perspective. Inman was that fortunate soul who has known, sought, and found his deepest desire. Placing his search into a time frame seems irrelevant. At a deep level, he dies a happy man. The novelist alludes to Ada only briefly, in a scene with her daughter. But the child symbolizes that Ada's desire was also identified, fulfilled, and lives on in a new form.

The Bridges of Madison County

A similar situation occurs in the novel and film *The Bridges of Madison County*. In a movie scene which resonates with archetypal overtones, the woman played by Meryl Streep tells her lover goodbye. While she is utterly caught up and transformed by her brief romance with him she chooses to remain with her husband

and children. Her decision is costly and painful; to some people it may be inexplicable. But the integrity of her action is validated years later, when she opens a package containing her lover's camera. During their long separation, she must have wondered if he had remembered her, or if their affair was as important to him as it was to her. His dying wish, to give her what was most important to him, brings a welcome "yes" to her questions.

Again, if we evaluate on a surface level, it might seem that her desire was as frustrated as Inman's. All the practical details may not have worked out; she wasn't permitted to live the rest of her life with the man she loved. But at another level, she knows who she is. She has been loved and has loved.

The previous two accounts are fiction and tell us of the human spirit in a way that only this art form can. The next example, however, is a true story. Cheryl's deepest desire was ordination to the priesthood. Many practical obstacles made this impossible: among them, she was a Catholic; her husband did not support the idea; she lacked the necessary education. Over time, however, Cheryl realized that even though she wasn't ordained in an official sense, she could find a priesthood of the heart. Her motivation and her service to other people could indeed be priestly. Now in her sixties, Cheryl is happy and fulfilled, as are many other people who call her their "priest."

Unachieved Desires: The Saints

A casual reader of these three examples might be puzzled. Why refer to people who didn't really achieve their deep desires? Each one seems thwarted, as did many of the saints. St. Ignatius of Loyola considered his desires graces from God. But he did not achieve the longing to spend his life in Jerusalem; he died in Rome. Nor did he become a Carthusian as he wished.

A similar survey of St. Francis's life shows serious conflicts dividing his brothers at the time of his death. When St. Clare suspected Francis was dying, she suffered terribly at the thought of not seeing him again. Francis sent word that she should not worry; she would see him again. Her desire was fulfilled in an ironic way: the brothers carried Francis's dead body to Clare's home.

Were these three saints thwarted? It may seem that they never achieved their desires, but sometimes identifying them is enough. Finding them leads to a solid peace, a glad assurance: "This is my truth, my best self. For this, God created me."

So we come full circle to the questions with which we began. How does the examination of desire connect with our struggles? Patricia O'Connell Killen explains that when we are both hungering for God and disillusioned with our religious heritage, we start a process of listening to our longing. Sometimes it's uncomfortable because it means taking ourselves and our lives seriously. "But it is vitally important to listen to our longings; for life, for others, for God. We are called to take ourselves seriously, genuinely to cherish ourselves as precious in God's eyes. Listening to our longings is the first step. Our longings are a place of intimate connection with our God because they also reveal God's longing for us."[56]

Our desires are not blind to androcentrism, patriarchy, or injustice. They are especially relevant to women's issues because "our longing is an affirmation that the Christian heritage is more than what it has said about and done to women up to now, more than the attitudes, words, behaviors, norms and rules embodied in current structures and expressed by some formally designated leaders."[57] Thus the whole process of articulating desire is an act of trust in those who have gone before us and those who will come after. It's our acknowledgement that this particular slice of church history isn't the whole pie. We sense a promise. And it starts within ourselves.

Well of Another Water

Where's your bucket, stranger? Are you
outcast too, asking a Samaritan for drink?
No idle well-side chat, this conversation costs.
You probe my pain; I yearn for your antidote.

Is it reproach or love, this splash of rain
after suffocating drought?
I rush to those who sneered at
me, and find them thirsty too.

Snug in my strength, like liquid
cupped in the well of his hands
I become the vessel for another spring
and a jar, abandoned, spins in dust.

14

Deep Wells

Reflection

Come, if you are willing, for an imaginary hike on the Platte River Greenbelt. It stretches for some twenty miles along a river in Colorado, with the Rocky Mountains in the distance beyond it. As we walk south, the mountains are a high, blue presence on the right. Ahead is Pike's Peak; the river is liquid silver beside us. It's a warm day in early September; the skies are clear. The sound of rushing waters fills the air, along with the droning of insects and the calls of a few birds. Wildflowers line the path: Indian paintbrush, purple daisies, clouds of Queen Anne's lace. It's a good day for a walk; our arms hang loosely and our steps move freely.

After a while, we start to tire and grow thirsty. Then we are in for a pleasant surprise. At intervals along the path, we come to rest stops. They have been built in memory of people who worked hard to establish this network of trails. Their families have created benches in the shade, water fountains, and plantings of flowers to honor the dead in a most appropriate way. So these places of refreshment are named, "Maria's Rest," "Carl's Rest," "Sarah's Rest."

Let's sit for a few minutes on a bench in the shade. As we watch the grasshoppers on the path and the ducks on the river, let's think about people who have come like surprises into our lives and provided us with rest. We may not even have known at the time that we needed them, but they came anyway, bringing shade in the heat, a cold drink, a bench when feet grew sore. They brought us beauty or balance when we needed it, challenge or humor when we needed that. If we think back over our lives as we would over this hiking trail, we can name places in their honor too. "Maria's Rest," "Carl's Rest," "Sarah's Rest."

What names do you remember and honor? What did these people provide?

When a tired Jesus sits down at the well (John 4:1–42), the action is richly resonant. When we sat in meditation at the rest stop described above, we relived his action. His human need for water echoes down into our day, but also resonates into the past. In his thirst, he is immediately surrounded by a cloud of witnesses, a long history of associations. As Gail Ramshaw points out: "In ancient times, in a dry land, the well was the town's meeting place, a locus for the community's exchanges, the place that death was traded for life."[58] Furthermore, it was the place where love was kindled, a backdrop for romance. Many Hebrew ancestors had met at the well: Jacob and Rachel, Moses and Zipporah; there Abraham's servant Eliezer finds Rebekah, a wife for Isaac. It was a life-saving place: when Hagar feared her son would die after they had been banished to the desert, God created a well (Gen. 21:9–21). Like any symbol, it embraces polarities: when the princes wanted to kill the prophet Jeremiah, they threw him into an empty well. "There was no water in the cistern, only mud, and Jeremiah sank into the mud" (Jer. 38:6). At times we can empathize with that metaphor.

In the story of the Samaritan woman, the well becomes even more than it has been in the past. She clearly knows the associations clustering around Jacob's well. Indeed, Jesus' request for water echoes Eliezer's plea to Rebekah, "Please let me sip a little water from your jar" (Gen. 24:17).

But the Samaritan woman wants more than the love sought by her matriarchs Rebekah and Rachel. At the well, as Ramshaw points out, they found their life's love; she has been unsatisfied in that quest.[59] The Song of Songs refers to the beloved as "a garden fountain, a well of living water, and flowing streams from Lebanon" (4:15). To build on the metaphor: for the Hebrew people, the word of God was a fountain. Jesus plays with the image as he speaks the word that quenches the thirst.

Woman at Work

That such an outpouring should come in the midst of an onerous chore might be the equivalent of someone today trekking to the grocery store and finding enlightenment among the canned soups. The woman is responding to a driving, physical need: she simply wants to fill her bucket and get home before it gets any hotter. She is completely surprised by an encounter which changes her life. The event reinforces the idea, recurrent in scripture, that splendid events *do* intersect the daily routine — at the well, not the synagogue; in the office, not the church; in the kitchen, not the temple. To those who feel distant or estranged from formal religion, it's good news that supposedly "unhallowed" ground is sacred.

The story spills over with more good news. The next encouraging note is how seriously Jesus takes the woman's desire, indeed teases it forth as he moves their discussion to deeper levels — at a time when no one else would consider it for a minute. Patriarchal religions hold up stories of women's desires with negative consequences: Eve and the apple, Herod's wife and the head of John the Baptist, the woman caught in adultery. These traditions say women's desire is bad unless guided and controlled by men.[60]

Before we scoff at such primitive societies, we should remember that contemporary women are often told not to want anything for themselves. Some defer their desires for years, often losing sight of their identities in the process. Others live out their longings through other people. They use spouse, clients, students, or children to fill their own unacknowledged desires.[61]

But Jesus recognizes and welcomes desire at the well. Indeed, he considers it more important than the task of carrying water — even more important than his own drink. Both the woman and Jesus find so much joy in their conversation that they forget the concerns that brought them to the well in the first place. He never gets his drink; she leaves behind her jar. As we saw in the previous chapter, the deep desires take precedence over the nagging daily concerns. Whatever hurts they have both suffered, whatever struggles they have had with the churches of Jerusalem and Samaria, they set them aside for this interlude. It may seem brief, but time becomes relative when it intersects the timeless.

Two-Part Dynamic: The Woman

Let's look in some depth at both the woman and Jesus. Ladies first: her response to Jesus is immediate and complete, as though he has tapped in her some flood that was bubbling close to the surface, waiting for the dam to burst. She doesn't stall a minute with the usual excuses: "It's a pretty busy weekend and the man I live with is waiting for his water. What you've said sounds interesting, but I'd better get home now. I'll get back to you on Monday." Nor does she cop out with the "we've always done it this way" excuse. "You must be new in town. Around here, women don't chat in public with strange Jewish men. Nor do we preach about God, upstaging the village elders! What kind of nerve do you think I have?"

Precisely — he has chosen her for her nerve. She responds intuitively and enthusiastically to a *promise:* after all, she never sees this miraculous water nor feels it spilling down her sleeves. It's all in his words, his voice, his presence, his style of call rather than coercion. That combination is powerful enough to drive her beyond the accepted social mores that have bound her all her life. There is something larger here; she senses it as clearly as rain in the air.

Perhaps she is freer to make this move because she has already questioned the taboos governing relationships with men. Risk-taking comes more naturally to her; she would not be afraid of an angel who troubles the waters (John 5), but might welcome the unpredictable. The intervention of God might destabilize the status quo, but it also brings marvelous surprises. One whose life has been filled with the topsy-turvy can welcome being caught off guard, left vulnerable and open to healing.

The fulfillment of her desires can come only after she has given them voice — and the story of women coming to voice is a longer one than can be told here.[62] Like many others touched by Jesus, she is different because of his influence: she comes into happiness. Like the magi who sought him in infancy, she must "return home by another way." She no longer skulks alone and anonymous to the well at noon, when no one else is there. She blazes into the village like a brass band, eager to speak her truth.

She speaks fluidly, enthusiastically, honestly, and so convincingly that the townspeople swallow their skepticism and run after her. Even the men, for a brief interlude, believe on the basis of her testimony. Then they quickly cover their tracks: "now we have come to believe on our own." But initially, she snagged them. She held them in the hollow of her hand. The power must have come from her words, demonstrating Etty Hillesum's idea: "We must only speak about the ultimate and most serious things in life when the words well up inside us as simply and as naturally as water from a spring."[63]

And Jesus

From Jesus' side of the story, the closest comparison is to a religious professional, a spiritual director or counselor, dedicated to her work for years. Then someone comes to see her whose thought or experience moves her to new insight. From the client or the directee, the counselor or director learns. It's a familiar dynamic to anyone involved in any kind of teaching; we learn more from our students than we ever begin to teach. When someone responds to our ideas in ways that stun and surprise us, our thoughts move to new levels we had not guessed nor foreseen.

While commentators extol the Samaritan's "missioning," evangelizing her village, the flood of her words is matched by an equal outpouring from Christ. After his encounter with her, he turns aside the disciples' more mundane concerns: physical food becomes secondary to the deeper nurture he has discovered.

We have probably all had the experience of meeting an extraordinary person, hearing a wonderful talk, or attending an inspiring retreat. We rush home to tell friends or family, who may listen politely for a minute or two, but then interject their concerns. "All very nice, but while you were gone, the car broke down." Or "the check bounced." Or "we called the plumber."

We feel then as Jesus must have felt. He goes on speaking, probably to himself, since he's clearly left the disciples behind. He changes from a water metaphor to a seed and harvest metaphor. Because of one woman who needed him, who responded eagerly and greedily to him, he can imagine a whole field shining ripe for the harvest. In one conversation with her, he was able to communicate what he was all about; he spoke of God's abundance and someone understood. He painted for her the picture of a gushing fountain, and she opened her soul to drink. Jesus becomes so excited about this encounter that he acts like one who has found his heart's desire. Indeed, he has: "I came that they might have life and have it to the fullest."

It was not a harvest he would ever see in reality. In his final hours, he might have hoped to see some justification for his life's work, some proof that all his teaching had borne fruit. When he looked down from the crucifix, he saw a faithful remnant, a little cluster of women. But he did not see what he had every right to expect, he who had sown good seed through brilliant teaching, who had healed countless people in compassionate miracle. He saw then no field of ripening wheat, no throng of followers.

But as we saw in the previous chapter, it's not necessarily *achieving* the desires that's important; it's the *discovery* that frees and exhilarates. Perhaps on Calvary, in the pain-filled haze of his consciousness stirred a memory: a woman's face reflected in water, a conversation, the faces in the future who would long for him.

The Two Meet

We have seen that we must take our desires seriously because they are the point of intersection with God's desires for us. The story of the well gives us an image for that intersection. In the blinding noon of a hot, dry climate, it is natural for the human eye to seek rest, coolness, refreshment. The eyes of both Jesus and the woman would be drawn to the watery, mysterious depths as a relief from the searing heat, just as people seek the shade beneath trees in summer. So, as they both turn toward the well, it is possible that peering into its deep violet depths, the Samaritan woman would see not only her own face, but Jesus' reflection as well. Perhaps their eyes met there before their gazes actually met.

In the purple shadows, the two fluid images mingle. Like any other symbol, this one is shifting, evocative, impossible to pin down. But it is rich in overtones. In the cool waters, desires meet too: her desire for God, God's desire for her. The whole conversation began, after all, with an overture from God: "Give me a drink." God sounds needy; God thirsts for her as, it becomes evident in the unfolding exchange, she thirsts deeply for God. John Shea describes this "match, a mutual desiring": "If we are interested in drinking from his well, his cupped hands offer us the water."[64]

"Listening to our longing evokes an act of faith from us…that we are of value, that we are worth the time and energy to notice our experience, to sit with it and to explore its meaning, trusting that God is with us in it."[65] Like Jesus at the well, we do not sit alone. The Samaritan woman is a model to us all of how to make that act of faith and "befriend our longing,"[66] moving past hurt to a deeper level of trust.

Emptiness Filled

That vacant place, that empty space where the bucket hovers before it touches water has been referred to metaphorically throughout spiritual literature. Those who stand in the lonely emptiness know they would never voluntarily seek out the place. Their struggles with their churches may have brought them here, against their wills, kicking and screaming. But like someone stuck overnight in a town that wasn't in the travel plans, they might as well look around and discover what's here.

What's here, the spiritual writers say, is great richness. The prophet Isaiah wrote uplifting promises for conflicted people:

> Though the mountains leave their place and the hills be
>   shaken,
> My love shall never leave you
> nor my covenant of peace be shaken,
> says the Lord, who has mercy on you.
> O afflicted one, storm-battered and unconsoled,
> I lay your pavements in carnelians
> and your foundations in sapphires:

I will make your battlements of rubies
your gates of carbuncles,
and all your walls of precious stones. (54:10–12)

Jesus continues this theme of empowering people: his saving grace transforms their storm-tossed affliction into rubies and sapphires. The woman at the well may have felt unconsoled by all her other relationships with men, but in this one she is made beautiful and whole. Whatever drudgery had been on her mind as she trudged to the well vanishes in a burst of insight and self-affirmation. She *runs* back to the village, her water jar symbolizing domestic duty left forgotten in the dust. She was made for greater things; she herself is vessel for the best news her villagers could ever hope to hear.

Your turn:

- For what do you thirst?

- Do you have any difficulty naming your deep longings? Why or why not?

- Do you think it's true that women especially are socialized not to want things for themselves? What does the Samaritan woman teach people about how to befriend their longings?

- Where are the wells in your life? Where do you enter conversations with God that fulfill and energize?

- What is calling you now, with the same intensity Jesus called to the woman at the well? Is it a relationship, a profession, a nagging injustice, an urge to creativity or community? What area in your life most needs the wellspring of his abundant waters?

15

The Search for a Viable Spirituality

PAULA

Risk-taking, honesty, and a playful humor characterize the Samaritan woman. Yet she was definitely an "outsider." Paula, who shares her qualities, would laugh at the labels. But she is definitely "in." It's becoming less ironic to find people who have serious reservations about the church holding key leadership positions within the institution. Perhaps those who are closest see the flaws; those at a distance are less troubled by them.

Paula holds a doctorate in Adult Education with an emphasis in Women's Studies, comes from a background in the United Methodist Church, and serves the national organization in a high-profile role. Yet she says softly, "One way of coping with the frustration is to withdraw from the local church. I'd join if I found one that meets my needs for spirituality and social justice.

"I've found other ways to nurture myself, but still haven't found a way to worship, which many people say is fundamental to faith. One experience that came close was celebrating Easter with three friends. Each one shared personal stories; we cracked open eggs, burned sage, and wished each other good new beginnings. In a simple way, it was worshipful, opening the self and listening to the struggles of the other.

"The lines between 'religious' and 'nonreligious' stuff are pretty hazy for me. I'm so steeped in how United Methodists do worship, church and life, that it becomes the internal norm. How could I capture the enthusiasm of the Latin American base communities, given the baggage I bring? How can I value my own experience enough to call it 'doing theology'? I have individually meaningful moments when writing or designing a meditation for an event, seeing how to modify a text for another context. Or doing the call to

87

worship during a workshop, with a Spirit-word that calls attention to what we're doing and why. I like showing people, 'This is soul work and this is why we're called to do it.'

"Maybe I want too much in a search for spirituality; maybe it's up to me, not the responsibility of the institution, to find it. So, too, I can create situations to empower women, but I can't do it for them. It's hard to admit I can only sow seeds.

"What deflates me in a traditional church setting are the emphasis on being told what to do and think, the disregard of women's talents and ideas, the exclusive language, and the disparity between what people say and how they live (of course acknowledging that's a problem for me personally as well).

"I dislike the current buzz word 'discernment.' How can anyone claim to discern the will of God for anyone but oneself? It's self-centeredness couched in theological language, to keep the laity out of the decision-making process. How can they argue with 'this is the will of God'? I've come to value my own thoughts as equally valid to someone's who has had hands laid on by everyone since Adam. Who's to say that if I don't go to church on Sunday to sing and pray, I don't have a chance to know God?

"When I've identified the life-draining forces, I can choose to avoid them and find other things. For me, it's reading feminist theology. For others, it may be dance or ritual. For poet May Sarton, it was the flowers in her garden and naming her alternate needs for solitude and company. Reading Shaman literature opens a whole new world: oneness with nature, expanded consciousness, healing of nature, sharing the perspective of an eagle or condor, these points on the edge of Christianity."

Like Jesus, she dismisses the ancient distinction between worship in Jerusalem and on Mt. Gerizim: "People's satisfaction with their spirituality comes from the inside, not from clergy or committee. But we must each figure out what gives us our spirit, how to find the awe in the everyday, name and celebrate places where we do make a difference, and not get caught up in an endless series of meetings and tasks.

"It's discouraging to see how much energy goes into maintaining traditional forms and preventing innovations. Surveys show a great spiritual hunger in people, but we haven't figured out how to make it alive and meaningful. Nor do we pay the professionals to do that. Despite all the effort that goes into maintaining the status quo, Luther happened. John Wesley happened. Small Christian communities are happening.

"It's hard to break out of the patterns of what people have been doing for hundreds of years — oriented toward religion, not spirituality. It's become so routinized that there's less emphasis on personal spiritual growth than on group process. People think they're doing important things: pie sales, rummage sales. Lots of contradictions and ambiguities are pushed aside. If the church really acted like church, we wouldn't have so much back-biting!

"It's easy for me to criticize the church. I need also to contribute to it the principles of adult education. We need to develop our critical thinking with regard to the church, and look at our basic assumptions:

- What do we expect?

- What values do we use to make decisions?

- Does what we do really follow from that?

"Process theology is open to surprise and novelty, while still acknowledging the residuals of sin and guilt. God changes as we change; God is fluid. Small groups working at the positives together may create a critical mass for something to emerge."

Paula is an intelligent and innovative seeker; one suspects that Jesus would enjoy a conversation with her beside a well. The church that someday learns to appreciate her talents and honor her insights will indeed be enriched.

16

A Long Drink of Compassion

J U L I A

People who thirst come to Julia because she is like a lake of serenity, a font of wisdom. Located at a counselling center that has offered a sane harbor to many, her office is an island of refuge. She's the Samaritan woman with an Irish accent and a Jewish spunk. Because she has identified her own longings with integrity, she can guide others to theirs.

"People come into my office," she begins quietly, "with horror stories. They are mortally wounded. They've been fired from church jobs for reasons that have nothing to do with performance. A new pastor has absolute power, so he dismisses all previous contracts. The bishop stands behind him, refusing to intervene because he won't contradict another's authority.

"That gets my Irish up. So first I shout, 'That's outrageous! It violates civil law as well as the gospel!' "

Then her voice softens. "After I explode, I ask 'So, how are you feeling?' They answer, 'worthless, dismissed, undervalued.'

"It's twice the wound because these arrogant authorities claim Christ and his way of life. In my tradition, an ingrown mentality says men are more important; they have something to say and women don't. Many women respect the church, but it doesn't respect them — unless they're in subservient or motherly roles.

"I stay in the church because of my belief in the mystery of Christ made present, for oneness with him and the community. But I've learn to stand apart from church, after once being at the heart of it. I know the hierarchy doesn't give life, so I step back, and the dance step could change often in a lifetime. It's a protective stance that says, 'I'm here, but not all of me. If this church is exclusive, then I can't be part of it.'

"We Catholics have been told there's no more discussion of women priests, as if authorities can tell us what to think and say! There's a better model for conflict. Look at the stand-off between Peter and Paul over the issue of Gentile circumcision (Acts 15). They prayed, they searched, they debated, they weighed evidence.

"Vatican Council II took the same approach: not 'truth will come from on high,' but 'let's look at everything and weigh it against the gospel.' Collegiality was the bedrock of Vatican II: the attitude of 'we do it all together' is a threat to absolute authority. In pictures, the Council fathers look like grim old men. But how much life came from their model!

"Church issues are like a marriage that's in trouble — you don't easily dismiss something precious and sacred. You consult the best minds, the experience of other people, struggle, confront and try to save what's good. Those who have been hurt are helped by others with similar experiences of being ignored, dismissed, and belittled. Then they get on with their lives: loving God and each other, taking care of the next generation and the planet. They admit, "This is the life I have. How do I live best in the midst of it?' The church may not be too exciting, but Christ is. So we keep loving, keep forgiving, keep eating and drinking that wonderful bread and wine."

Julia describes the meaning of compassion through a true story. "A class of children with Down's syndrome were having a party for some in their group who were graduating to the next level. One little girl was so damaged that her only way to demonstrate affection was to blow puffs of air into someone's face. She didn't quite understand that her friends would be leaving until she got to the party.

"Then she began to wail uncontrollably. Two other children ran for tissues, another patted her back, but one child blew puffs of air in her face. . . . That is, I guess, how we learn God's compassion. Forgiveness is sometimes beyond our hearts. But it's not beyond God's heart."

Perhaps the story of the Down's syndrome children is a gospel in itself. The child who blew air puffs to comfort a little girl is like Christ who learned our stunted language, no words but a wail. We were so pathetically limited, we had no vocabulary for affection. Yet he taught us one and cured us.

Julia's compassion springs from her own experience of hurt and struggle. She has entered into the dilemmas others describe, but she has also learned to step back from them. Her calm assuages thirst and assures people they can face anything.

17

The Blue-Green Solace of Nature

While the solace of nature has long been touted by romantic poets and environmentalists, it may hold a special healing for those who struggle with their churches. Entering God's spacious creation restores a freedom and peace we may not know we've lost. Nature offers a wider view, in which we realize that petty issues have grown great in our own minds, mushroomed out of all proportion to what's really important. A starry sky dwarfs our puny concerns, or at least helps us set them aside for a while.

Aching and tired, we can step into a world where the elk cavort in daisy-speckled meadows and the moose nuzzling silver streams step delicately into pools of sunset. The trout in an explosion of droplets leaps into the air after a mosquito, and the colors themselves soothe: the lupine shadows of clouds on hillsides or the mossy reflections of trees in lakes. In the gray-green quiet of forest swirls a mystery that few churches can capture.

In the celebratory rush of many waters, we hear how abundant grace might sound. The promise resounds, engraved on sinew, etched on bone, echoed in ear: through you surge the waters of eternal life. In the protection of tiny red mushroom caps sheltering frail moss we see God's reminder: I will never forsake you.

We slide into happiness as into a favorite robe, cotton and soft. The tension drains away, one sleeve at a time. The face becomes absorbed, the shoulders relax, a smile plays at the corners of the mouth. In some mysterious way, we are restored to Eden. It's a good time to recall the ancient Chinese proverb:

> Tension is who you think you should be;
> relaxation is who you are.

There are places where children jump into blue lakes and their skin shivers; there are places within us where we are children still. In that inner sanctum, our only concerns are breathing a lungful of clover warmed by the sun, or studying the pattern of tree limbs against the sky. Such an action recalls Walter Burghardt's definition of contemplation: "a long, loving look at the real."

Surrounded by creation and steeped in beauty, the soul can unfold and blossom. Just as we must be relaxed enough to sleep, so the world of nature puts us in the frame of mind to receive God's gifts. Then we enter that peace the poet Rumi describes:

> Something opens our wings. Something
> makes boredom and hurt disappear.
> Someone fills the cup in front of us.
> We taste only sacredness.[67]

Our happiness becomes intense enough to drive out the frustration and anger and stupidity — or at least modify them to a bearable degree. In an inversion of the Sermon on the Mount, we respond to God's generous offer: "It is the little flock's good pleasure to seize the kingdom."

Perhaps the example of one ordinary morning will show God's gracious working through nature. Eavesdropping on a personal journal or conversation, we might find something like this:

It rained about 5:00 this morning, the sound cascading softly on the roof, wrapping us even more securely in sleep. I went out for a walk around 8:30, when the skies had cleared, but the smell of the rain remained, caught like tissue in the leaves, heightening and freshening the plant aromas. I walked like one drunk on smells, sniffing every flower, every light green tip of darker pine bough. Little jewels of rain were left everywhere like a trail of pollen, caught especially in clusters of leaves, where one drop balanced precisely in the center of a cup like a diamond in its setting.

Sometimes one sees the perfect solitaire, where a diamond is not surrounded by other flashy jewels, but stands alone, lovely in its simplicity. Sometimes a woman with taste wears a simple diamond stud in her ear, confident that's all the jewelry she needs. The leaf-cups with their clear centers magnifying the green veins beneath had that kind of simplicity.

The soul must be like that, somehow. The legends of many peoples speak of the divine spark in humans, clear and beautiful, placed precisely at the center. Around us chaos may rage, but that still place remains inviolate, a point which the Quakers call "that of God" in each person.[68]

What of the hurts and harms done to people? Perhaps natural defenses close themselves like petals around the inner jewel, protecting the divine spark. For unlike the flower which freezes or the drop of water which evaporates, the human spirit continues, the diamond burns within. For some people who have been terribly hurt, waiting outlasts hope. Them seem to experience only silence, paralysis.

The emptiness might be compared to the childlessness of the scriptural figures Zechariah and Elizabeth (Luke 1:5–24, 57–80). They wait so long for a baby that when the good news of pregnancy finally comes, Zechariah reacts not with joy but with skepticism. Because of his doubt, he is struck dumb for nine months. We know little of Elizabeth, her maternal anticipation overshadowed by his glum silence. But we suspect that into that stillness Mary's Magnificat must have poured, welcome as music.

And, as Melissa Nussbaum points out, Zechariah's song (Luke 1:68–79) is eventually born from that silence.[69] Leaving that zone of incubation, that quiet cocoon, the first words he writes are, "His name is John," a name meaning "God is gracious." Zechariah models for us that even people who have lost hope in a waiting that has dragged on too long, even people caught in the silence of their own skepticism can refocus on the jewel, the spark of divine life within.

It may seem like a long leap from a leaf holding a drop of water to the canticle of Zechariah. But those attuned to nature know that it can be the springboard for imaginative journeys and for prayer. We know too that we can always return to this place of solace. If we visit there often enough, it stays in the mind.

When we are in darkness, we know with certainty that somewhere the moon trails its silvery path across a lake and the stars are swimming in purple velvet. Then we can say in the words of the Chinook Psalter:

> Thou hast filled all places with thy beauty.
> May all creation dance within me.

Your turn:

- Deliberately spend an hour outdoors, preferably in a beautiful setting of plants, flowing water, and spacious skies. What do you learn from creation about the creator? How does your soul respond to an experience of nature?

– Part IV –

Nurture and Healing

There is a secret medicine
given only to those who hurt so hard
they can't hope.

The hopers would feel slighted if they knew.

— RUMI

Nurture

No matter what we name it, the struggle is always an attempt to make sense of our own lives. Whether the foil of the moment is the church, the boss, the sibling, or the spouse, we are always cast back on the same old self and inner resources. Whatever the particular struggle, the soul needs the same nurture: tenderness, compassion, meaning, the abiding presence of God.

During a struggle with the church, we turn to images of healing and nurture because we operate out of our images of the church. These are so important we can't allow anyone else to control them. Others may try to make their images the operative ones: e.g., the church as hierarchy, defender of orthodoxy, exclusionary fortress of truth. If we concede to those voices, if we do not work out of the images that feed and challenge us, then our spiritual lives are impoverished and we have little to share with others.

So we turn to the best biblical sources that have replenished seekers across the centuries: the deep wells of the previous section, the charcoal fires of this one. Next we see how two people have responded to Christ's invitation: cast the nets to the other side, get warm, eat breakfast by the fire. If we can imagine fishermen doing a jig with delight at a large, unexpected catch, we can draw together biblical and contemporary sources. We can imagine that dance step reflected in the lives of people interviewed here.

During a struggle, turning to nurturing images like the well and the fire protects us from striking out in meanness. We ask, "Where do I find that scene of well or picnic in my life today?" then burrow deeply into the image and draw forth its graces.

Healing

Just as the postresurrection picnic continued the pattern of Jesus eating many meals with his friends, so the pattern of healing was consistent throughout his ministry. Our own need for a cure is personified by three characters in varying forms of distress who cross the gospel stage. They are icons for our present or past situations, three steps along a spectrum:

> the bent woman
> the paralyzed man
> the dead child.

Perhaps we are weighed down by indifference or exhaustion, bent beneath the weight of injustice. Perhaps we are paralyzed, so badly hurt that we are unable to move forward ourselves; we must rely on the initiative of friends. Or perhaps some part of us is dead, sunk into depression, so lost we think we can never rise again. In identifying with one or all of the three biblical figures completely or partially, we can also identify with their healing. The questions after each meditation are designed to draw us into that process of relating and rising.

The stories of Barbara and Mark do not relate physical healings, but inner, spiritual ones. After paralyzing encounters with the church, they have both returned gradually to an upright posture, movement forward, and praise for a God who is larger than they knew before. With sadness, Luke diagnoses serious symptoms in the church he cares about passionately.

18

Charcoal Fires

Reflection

Smell fresh wind across a lake and the lazy spiral of wood smoke. Hear the thump of waves against a wooden boat, the shouts of old friends across the waters. Feel the warmth of bread, the sinews of fishing nets. See nets bulging with fish, wet scales flashing silver in the sun, gills heaving and tails thrashing. Look up at the dawn traces of salmon and apricot streaking the papery white sky. Rub elbows with the crew gathered around the fire, smelling like fish, toasting their backsides, roaring their jokes. Taste fish freshly caught and grilled. Feel the satisfaction of food after hunger, rest after a long night's work. Dwell in the comfort of a beloved face.

•

The story of Jesus' postresurrection breakfast picnic (John 21:1–14) is rich in homey detail, which nurtures at the most basic sensate level, even before we explore its deeper themes. Dom Helder Camara, archbishop of Recife, Brazil, says of this gospel passage: "I like these little details: the Lord had already lit the fire, ready to cook the fish. The Lord is just as considerate after his resurrection as before. . . . I love God's delicacy of touch."[70]

The details help set a scene which is crucial to the story's theme. Again, the action begins when the key characters are at work, not in church. Like the Samaritan woman, the disciples are engaged in a daily chore, wanting to satisfy the basic need for food. Like ourselves, sometimes wanting only to get through a day without crisis, they are unprepared for the avalanche of grace they receive. After a whole night of catching no fish, the note of despair creeps in, as it did for the Samaritan woman. She does not speak directly of her fatigue, but we can hear her hope stirring when she says, "Sir . . . Give me some of that water, so that I may never get thirsty and never have to come here again to draw water" (John 4:15). We can only imagine the slumped shoulders, clammy clothing, and bleary eyes suggested by the phrase "[they] caught nothing that night" (John 21:3).

In response to their need, Jesus does not appear in the temple precincts, give a lecture on law, or hand out a book of dogma. Jerusalem, center of Jewish civic and religious life, had not been a happy place for any of them. So he does not meet them there. Instead, Jesus meets his friends on a shore where he feeds them in a setting of abundance and beauty, with the dawn glinting off the lake's pewter surface.

The names in the cast of characters are evocative. They stir memories of other needs at other times: Nathaniel from Cana in Galilee (where "they had no more wine"), the sons of Zebedee (whose mother wanted her boys to get the perks of the apostle job), Thomas the Twin, who, after the struggle recounted in Part II, has regained his place in the company.

Tired after such a sleepless, unproductive time, their garments hanging heavy with moisture, the disciples squint through the morning mist at a stranger on shore. They lean forward with a genuine, gut-level need, not the phony needs church leaders sometimes think people have: for absolute certainty, advice that skirts the complexities of life, liturgical purity. (Did that bread Jesus offer contain unsanctioned honey or whole wheat flour? And who approved *fish* for a eucharistic celebration?)

It is not hard to identify with these characters in their gutsy, human need. Sometimes, we are like Peter, so sunk in depression that all he can do is plod numbly through routine. He has betrayed his best friend, who'd undergone torture and a criminal's execution. For all he knew, he would never see him again, and guilt would haunt the rest of his life. His hopes crushed, he returns to the one sure thing, the steady rhythm of casting out and hauling in, the job he had known longer than he had known Jesus. He looks to the familiar rut to help him bury the bright promise. Potential that had once flared now lies in ashes.

For Peter as for the Samaritan woman, abundant life bubbles up in the vacuum of great need. If we sense within ourselves a void corresponding to theirs, we too can lean forward intently. The space can become sanctuary. The place of emptiness is also the place of transcendence. With God, there is never the niggling, hanging-back hesitance, always the full, brash outpouring.

So in one splendid instant, hope is restored. The vehemence with which Peter hurls himself into the water says something about Peter and something about God. Peter was not one to cower in the bottom of the boat; his huge splash probably drenched everyone in it. Once before he had plunged into the lake at Jesus' invitation, but sank when he realized he couldn't walk on water. Peter gets his second chance here — or is it the third or fourth?

Anyone who grows irritated with church pomposity must savor the moment when the bumbling oaf (and first pope) throws on his cloak, an action just the opposite of most people jumping in a lake. Did he (or a later editor) think impulsively, "Better come clothed to Jesus," or "grab clothes for history"? Would later generations, attired in Sunday clothes, scratchy shirts, hot suits, and dressy shoes hear this gospel and envy Peter?

So much for what the passage tells of Peter. What does it tell of God? Jim Dunning explains that the scene is one of "healing memories," showing "how a broken past can resurface and be redeemed."[71] When Peter approaches the charcoal fire, he cannot forget that other charcoal fire in the high priest's courtyard, where he swore his triple denial. Yet the place of betrayal becomes a scene of blessing. There seems to be nothing Jesus cannot forgive. He does not berate Peter; he feeds him. His gentle invitation, "Come and eat breakfast," sounds like a mother calling to children. He does not trumpet his presence after the resurrection as some might, with Swiss guards, banners, swords, and the Tabernacle Choir.

Furthermore, scripture scholars tell us, there is no hierarchy at his table. In preparing and serving food, he does what in his culture was "women's work." Furthermore, all eat the same food — even one whose body is resurrected. Jesus' model stands as a corrective to churches who have become more concerned with barring people from the table than welcoming them to it. He invites the people's

contributions, not spurning them because they are female or gay/
lesbian or divorced/remarried or members of "another" denomination. He asks their involvement: "Bring some of the fish *you have
just caught*" (John 21:10). He probably could have created all the
fish they needed, but sensitive to their dignity, he invites their labor, their ownership. They, after all, hauled in the heavy nets and
dragged them ashore.

Perhaps most relevant to those engaged in the struggle over
church is the way they respond to the directive, "Throw the net out
to starboard and you'll find something" (John 21:6). Sometimes it
is painful to shift the net to the other side; our perceptions, work,
and mind-sets are firmly established. No matter how desolate the
waters have become, we stubbornly continue to fish them. Even at
the cost of our best selves, we remain in denial. We may criticize
entrenched authority for the tired defense, "We've always done it
this way!" But the same hackneyed cliché often rises awkwardly to
our own lips.

Once before, Peter had been skunked (Luke 5:1–11) and responded, "Master, we have worked all night long but have caught
nothing. Yet if you say so, I will let down the nets." Such a
spirit might encourage us when we fish hostile lakes. Peter's attitude invites God's grace when the situation looks hopeless, the
relationship seems barren, the labor appears fruitless, the work is
undervalued. Fish may flicker in the most dismal-looking lakes.

Surely a prison is an unlikely setting to exemplify the gospel
lived out today. But it's hard not to draw the parallels when Sister Helen Prejean describes the last supper of an inmate on death
row. She eats that meal with Dobie Williams, the man condemned
to death, and tells of an occurrence as stunning as catching 153
big fish. "And, miracle of miracles, unbelievable God-swooping-in-
amazing grace, the warden comes into the room to tell Dobie of
the stay of execution just as the fried shrimp and catfish are being
served."[72]

The overtones of eucharistic banquet ring clear despite the im-
probable setting: "Dobie invited two guards who had been with us
all day in the death house to join us and two of his lawyers who
were there, and we all sat and ate and marveled and wondered and

ate and laughed, and it was a meal like no other meal."[73] There is even a "doggie bag" of leftover fish to share with all the other death row inmates. It's interesting to note that Prejean's dramatic experience of "this amazing Gospel"[74] would never have happened had she pursued the more traditional, officially approved roles of Catholic nuns, which critics would like to force her into.

In the section that follows, let's look at people who risked a cast to the other side — and the riches they found there.

Your turn:

- What image from this story appeals most to your senses: the smell of campfire smoke, the light traces of dawn brushing the pale sky, the slap of wave against wooden boat, the taste of bread and fish, the sound of voices?

- Where are the "charcoal fires" in your life? Where do you find an easy, nurturing companionship with Christ and his friends that parallels that of the gospel?

- Do you ever sense the call to cast your net in a different direction? Where might Jesus be leading you next?

19

"Come and Have Breakfast"

C A R A

It is easy to recall the maternal words and gesture of Jesus beside the lake when Cara leads people in prayer. Presiding at the Eucharist, she opens her arms in a gesture suggesting a wide embrace. Warmly she says, "All are welcome at this table." At a time when some denominations quibble over who can come to the table, Cara's words echo with a reassuring similarity to the words of Jesus.

An ordained minister in the United Church of Christ, an author, spiritual director, and seminary professor, Cara is poised, articulate, creative. At a retreat house in autumn, she invites people to gather for morning prayer near an eastern window. Just as the sun's rays strike a crimson maple, she offers reverent praise for creation. Once again, the little band of disciples gathers at dawn around their leader.

She does not disappoint them. People of all denominations long for Cara's style of openness and inclusion; members of many faith traditions come to her for spiritual direction.

Soul-Nurture

She explains her work in this field: "When I see people for spiritual direction, I have the expectation that they be in a worshiping community. Notice, I didn't say a *perfect* community. Some people find they need communi*ties* or churche*s* in the plural. A wandering churchgoing style may meet different needs: where one church alone fails to nurture, several combined may be life-giving. Just as no one person can meet all our needs, so too with churches. There's no disloyalty here, simply being responsible in exploring.

"I find people exploring new language for God, seeking new ways to do ritual. They're asking questions like this: While staying connected to symbolic language and traditional ritual, how can we transform them? Maybe it's a question of how to scrape off the barnacles! People long to know they aren't the only seekers; they want companionship and affirmation. They wrestle with church teaching on divorce and gender orientation. They want help in taking care of their bodies, which in turn nourish their souls. People can't do their own transformation; they look to the church for ways to connect to the universe. They're also searching for ways to lighten up: how do they bring humor and play into the spiritual life?"

Food for the Struggle

Asked specifically about advice for people who struggle with their churches, Cara responds: "The struggle in my church may be a little different than people have in hierarchical ones. We have congregational polity, which means that the final authority lies in the congregation. While the goal of this system is to restrict unbridled power, a group can also be abusive and power-hungry. But usually it's not as blatant as a rigid hierarchy!

"The worse problem, which it sometimes leads to instead, is rampant incompetence. We've never answered the question, 'Who are the gatekeepers?' Consequently, time and money get wasted; hearts are broken. An elderly minister may be denied a church for good reasons, but surely he has the right to know why. In this system, there's no clear-cut answer, no final authority to tell him.

"For most people in the pews, the hurt isn't as grave as it is for professional ministers, because the church is irrelevant. It isn't answering the questions they're asking. Oh, a few pockets here and there may address the real issues, but most don't.

"Some people who are seriously hurt may be those who want to grow beyond a conforming stage of development. They want to become more inclusive, but the church points a threatening finger and resorts to, 'But the Bible says....' Consequently, they learn that if they're going to grow, they must leave the church. Sure, the church comes across as warm and accepting — till you begin to question!

"I'm a firm believer in process theology. That means the church is in process too, always moving toward greater goodness, wholeness and healing. I can participate in its transformation: affirming hopeful things, helping healthy initiatives, challenging indications of regression."

Her last words of advice for those who struggle come with contemplative serenity: "Breathe. Just keep breathing. Ask 'where's the gift here?' "

In her own way, Cara is gift to the Christian community. Standing at the altar in a linen alb, the lace around her collar the same soft white as her hair, she is a welcome sight. People are drawn to her just as once they rushed ashore to a stranger cooking fish over an open fire.

20

Parallel Patterns

SCOTT

The parallels between Scott's ministry and the scene of the charcoal fire emerge at every turn in the two stories. The themes move together like those in music: suffering the passion, gathering the community, feeding the beloved people.

The pastoral associate in a large Catholic parish, Scott takes on many roles which were once the domain of the ordained clergy. He directs religious education, sacramental preparation, and a corps of catechists. Yet Scott ministers from a different context: the father of two, he is deeply committed to his wife and children. Clearly his family is a primary commitment that affects all he does. To a church with a celibate leadership, he brings the refreshing perspective of a caring husband and dedicated dad.

Suffering the Passion

Before coming to his present position in parish ministry, Scott had served on the faculty at the diocesan seminary run by order priests. The diocese took it over because they needed the space for their own chancery offices. Furthermore, they objected to the faculty's teaching "radical" theologians like Jesuit Karl Rahner and educating many more lay students than candidates for the ordained priesthood. When the seminary closed, students who had begun graduate degrees were left in mid-program; many fine teachers lost their jobs. Several years after the closing, Scott reflected on its impact:

"The diocese's abrupt and final action was an invasion of the spirit that permeated the place. I felt like Captain Von Trapp in the movie *Sound of Music*, when he returns from his honeymoon and finds the Nazi flag flying over his home. But they can't erase the memories. They can't take over a place that meant so much to so many people.

"While diocesan officials claimed there was a financial crisis, their decision was strictly political. They didn't like the teaching they considered liberal and took quite seriously the negative comments of a few seminarians, who aren't even seminarians anymore. The faculty were aware of some financial difficulties, so we'd begun alternate programs and had assured the school of a high ranking in the accreditation process. The final decision, made without consultation and handed down from on high, was a slap in the face of the faculty and the order who had run the place for years."

In his present position, Scott must still deal with the chancery officials responsible for closing the school that had meant so much to him. The relationship is an ongoing struggle, but he has learned to cope with the hierarchy: "I don't attend diocesan meetings because they don't impact what I do. I choose not to be in relationship with them because they don't get it, don't know what it means to be in the trenches. I choose to be in relationship with other ministers who do understand.

"For instance, the diocese hired a person as director of youth ministry who'd had only one year of experience at a parish. They were impressed by his college credentials. The same thing happened with the diocesan director of initiation, who knows nothing about the process, but graduated from a conservative school.

"Consequently, such people talk a great program, but don't know what's happening. They tried to introduce a program on sexuality: fifteen sessions. Don't they realize we have the kids for only twenty sessions? Sure, I'll try to implement some of what they want, but I don't plan to spend the entire year on sex education — there's so much more to the faith than sexuality."

The disciples, exhausted and bruised by their experience of Christ's passion, sought comfort in each other and the familiar routines of work. So Scott, having suffered with Christ, has found ways to rise with him: work with a faith community has been one path.

Gathering the Community

"Sure, closing the seminary hurt, but the blessing was that it brought me to my current job. I'm in a lively, educated community that calls forth different gifts. I no longer look at the big picture of church, but at the people we minister with. I try to disconnect from politics and trust in the Spirit. Is any battle really worthwhile? I try to pray about issues, then be at peace.

"But that doesn't mean I won't be an advocate. If I don't like a decision one time, I learn how to approach it better next time. The hierarchs play their games — I did it once too. Let them push their papers around and play politics. But they'd be amazed and excited if they really saw faith in action, if they really knew the people they're praying with, rather than watching it from a window (or an altar). How hard that must be for someone like an archbishop, with all the demands made on him."

After many struggles, Scott can laugh with healthy humor about his ecclesiastical employer: "Sure, the church is corrupt, but we keep it going. Like the government — it's falling apart, but we still pay taxes!" The realism that permeates the story of the breakfast picnic pervades Scott's story too. He does not look at ministry through rosy frames, but sees its tough challenges.

"I'm always asking myself, 'When do I act like the Good Samaritan and when should I walk on by? How do I balance my needs and those of my family against those of the community?' Sometimes I feel like I need to be accessible twenty-four hours a day — and the weekends are murder!

"When I try to protect myself and say no, it worries me, because people see that as God saying no. Yet I also know there's nothing worse than a burnt-out minister. What kind of modeling is that? There are too many people out there who hate their jobs and families — I don't want to be one more. I want to be the messenger of hope. I want to be at peace with myself and God, take time for prayer, find balance in my life, take care of myself so I can be vibrant. I want to live out the passage in 1 Corinthians about faith, hope, and love, where it says that love is the one thing that abides.

"There's more demand on ministers today than ever before.

People used to call the church only when they were dying, but now there's a greater openness, not as much fear; they call us all the time. It's what we're here for. We wanted them to think for themselves and come to us, yet the demands are increasing at the same time that the number of priests is decreasing. Lay ministers like myself pick up most of the slack. I remind myself that the church isn't my whole life; that helps keep my sanity when it gets crazy."

Like Peter fishing without his clothes, Scott is quick to dismiss any self-righteousness. "I worry that sometimes I get hierarchical myself about imposing requirements on people rather than reverencing people's innate spirituality. Does the class I teach on baptism make people better parents? I hope so. I think the educational piece is important, but am I insisting on it too much?"

Feeding the Beloved People

The pattern of Scott's work echoes in his home: the suffering, the community, the nurture. His thirteen-year-old son Dan, born with spina bifida, has had over forty surgeries, the last one painful and extensive. At a time when Dan was eager to start junior high, he was instead in recuperation for six months when movement was severely restricted.

"My wife, Susan, just goes through the motions of religious practice. She can't resolve how a good God could allow so much suffering to happen to our son. She keeps asking, 'Hasn't Dan been through enough?' I suspect that Susan's love/hate relationship with God may be deeper than the relationships of those who have never faced a crisis. She's going through a dark night of the soul, but knows that if conversion is going to come, it will come through the faith. So she waits.

"Her grandpa built their parish church and lived across the street from it. Her dad and brothers were heavily involved with the parish: playing the music, plowing the snow, ringing the bells. Her husband and kids are excited about the church and spend lots of their time there, but her heart's not in it. Growing up in an active Catholic family, still being in one, yet being detached — it's almost like being at a party where everyone else is pleasantly tipsy, and you're the only one who's sober.

"I pray that Susan can reconnect someday, maybe through a liturgy or an Easter Vigil, but I'm afraid to get her hopes up again. She's afraid God will disappoint her. Dan's in a wheelchair, but she's paralyzed inside. She doesn't want to step out on the water in faith again."

Scott probably isn't aware that his metaphor is so fitting, or that the themes of his life are so closely intertwined with scripture. Yet a note of resurrection sounds clear in his voice: "We keep going because of the hope. We've had the miracles before; we look forward to them again. But for those who don't experience those high points, the hurts simply break the heart even more. For these people, the answer doesn't lie in words, but in relationships, actions, opening ourselves to God in others."

Simon, son of John, do you love me?...Feed my sheep.

(John 21:16, 17)

Of Spirits and Spines

Bending double could impair perspective:
sky's leap or star's plume could buckle.
The rain known by smell, not by clouds,
the trees by roots, not by leaves and
people not by faces, but by feet.
In eighteen years, her child grew tall
as green stalk: she watched from an angle.

The call, the touch, the freeing words like
breeze on her uplifted face. Twisted
spine straightens slowly as a morning stretch
or a tendril uncurling in sun. Her fixed stare
on gravelly ground turns to him: first sight,
the clean kiss of what she was meant to be.
With buoyant posture, she looks into his eyes.

Blind to the pearled line of her straight spine,
the leaders bend double to quibble, contorted by
questions: Why not cure on the other six days?
Isn't healing on the sabbath blasphemy? He nails
their cruelty: you easily water ox or donkey, yet
you deny her. Today she bends; still she waits words
to clink like keys in the rusty lock of her bondage.

21

The Bent Woman

(L U K E   1 3 : 1 0 – 1 7)

A personal request prompted other miracles, but Jesus does not wait for this woman to ask. His action is immediate: "When Jesus saw her, he called her over and said, 'Woman, you are set free from your ailment'" (Luke 13:12). Most people at the synagogue that day would see a pathetic, crippled woman almost lost in a crowd. Jesus sees past the appearance of infirmity to the child of God. In his splendid vision, God's daughter stands erect and tall, as she was meant at her creation.

The power of his dream for her is so intense that her cure is instantaneous: "When he laid his hands on her, immediately she stood up straight and began praising God" (v. 13). That movement is a dance of joy, a shimmer along the spine, a beauty in her graceful rising. But we are barely given time to enjoy the moment of praise before the church officials break in, quibbling.

The protest does not sound unfamiliar: we too have heard the tirades about trivia from the same source. But all who grow discouraged with church officials can take heart from Jesus. He does not waver; uncowed by religious authority, he boldly confronts their hypocrisy. He names their cruelty for what it is: a failure to provide a woman with the same dignity they would accord an ox. We can almost hear the trumpets blare as his opponents are put to shame and the crowd goes wild with rejoicing. When the victories seem few, we can cherish those that are this sweet.

Your turn:

- What causes you to feel bent over?

- Are the forces that weigh you down internal? external?

- Where do you seek Jesus' healing touch that restores you to standing upright?

22

Believing in "Divine Guile"

BARB

Barb stands tall after an ordeal that could have crippled her. Betrayed by one of her staff because of her position on artificial birth control, she lost her job at a diocesan level. In retrospect, she reflects, "Someday, the *sensus fidelium* ["sense of the faithful"] will prevail on this issue, but not before more anguish, heartache, and injustice occurs, I am afraid."

A thoughtful woman of fifty, Barb speaks with hard-won personal conviction about the birth control issue which has long polarized the Catholic Church. Many left the church or the ordained priesthood when *Humanae vitae* appeared. This papal document condemned the use of any means of birth control other than the rhythm method. Other Catholics remained and worked through an arduous conflict between authority and conscience.

Caught in the Controversy

Over time, the matter ceased to be a major issue for most married couples. Only the hierarchy seemed insistent that adherence to official teaching was the litmus test of orthodoxy. And in that controversy, Barb got caught. While she had resolved the issue for herself, it came back to haunt her when she got a job doing the work she loved at a diocesan level: working toward economic justice, in prison ministry and for immigrants to her border state. She tells her story:

"When I was six, my mom was diagnosed with diabetes. The doctor warned that having any more children could kill her. I had a three-year-old brother and a one-year-old sister at the time. Mom and Dad anguished over what to do and went to the parish priest.

He told them the only method of birth control they could practice was distance and resistance, so they bought twin beds.

"That constant pressure, combined with financial stress, led my dad to become an alcoholic. Their sex life became furtive and fearful, its frequency measured by the thermometer. After she went through menopause, they got a queen-sized bed again, but by that time they had missed out on twenty years of married intimacy. They had become skilled at distance and resistance.

"I was about fifteen when Mom explained the church's teaching on birth control. It didn't make sense then and nothing since — including eighteen years of Catholic education and training in critical thinking — has changed my mind. When I married at twenty-one, I told my husband that our need for and right to sexual intimacy was more important to me than church teaching about birth control. We have four wonderful, planned children, and would have welcomed any unplanned ones.

"When I completed my master's degree in theology, I took a job working for the diocese on social justice issues. I never publicly dissented from *Humanae vitae,* but in a private conversation outside the workplace, I said I didn't think the pope should tell African women who were so malnourished they couldn't breast-feed the babies they had that artificial birth control was intrinsically evil. I think that asking married couples to choose between the embrace of their beloved and church teaching is wrong.

"One of my staff members who overheard the conversation wrote a letter to the national pro-life office saying that I had dissented from *Humanae vitae.* I wasn't allowed to read her letter, but I was asked to resign or be fired because of my *public* dissent. The diocesan lawyer and bishop sat in on my hearing, where I questioned their response to an act of betrayal from my own staff."

Betrayed and Fired

"The same bishop who had publicly praised my stands on peace and justice informed me that 'you are no longer suitable or worthy to occupy a teaching office in the diocese.' Although he assured me that someone with my own passion and priorities would be hired to take my place, I was deluded again. My replacement had little interest in the church's social ministry, only a burning commitment to 'orthodoxy.' Talk about straining after gnats and swallowing camels: I just can't believe our bishops are still doing this dance after thirty years!

"They also ignore the lived experience of millions of Catholic couples trying to remain faithful to each other and the teachings of Jesus in turbulent times. Many people wrote the bishop expressing their outrage at how I was treated. I was out of work for eighteen months and became clinically depressed. My family suffered serious economic loss; one son almost had to drop out of college. Finally, I found a job I like, though I make $8000 less than I did at the diocese! The whole experience made me a great believer in the divine guile — how God brings good from evil.

"I still voice and act out my passion for justice, especially through ministry to immigrants. 'When I was a stranger, you welcomed me' seems more a gospel truth than whether or not married couples are charting the wife's temperature and observing the viscosity of her vaginal secretions. Maybe the bishops can explain what's natural about that! It seems to me that married love is spontaneous and freely shared like precious nard, not something parceled out frugally according to some schedule.

"To me, some church teaching smacks of idolatry. Only God is worthy and deserving of our ultimate loyalty, not church law or any human law which violates human dignity. That's what I got from Catholic education and Catholic faith, and that's why social justice issues are so important to me. I will be disappointed when and if I reach the heavenly gates to find out that the yardstick for acceptance is sexual behavior, orientation, and one's unquestioning submission to 'orthodoxy.' Meanwhile, our bishop is silent on welfare reform and fails to protest the atrocities to immigrants at the border." In her ministry to these, Barb stands straight and praises God.

Flying Carpet: Capernaum

No more jokes, my crazy friends!
Did you plot this over a six-pack,
when I dozed during poker last night?
I've had it with your pranks. I don't trust
your Boy Scout knots or pulleys that hold me
dangling in mid-air, swaying above the crowd.

It's a hoot to you: hoisting me to the roof,
digging a hole, the heave-ho, wobbly ride, people
squinting in sudden light, expecting angels. I foil
hope; I, an insect pinned with splayed wings.
Your silly noose softens and I thud to ground,
look into eyes amused and grin big as a skirt.

"What flying beast have I netted now?" he'd ask
if irony wouldn't stun. This bird is grounded;
this flight halts in the swamp of my paralysis.
Set jokes aside and friends' bets off:
I'm stuck, resigned, petrified as stump.
One problem, pals: mistaking your desire for mine.

I balk at the call to move — bad joke gone sour.
Faces crowd the opening overhead; buddies
jostling for the best view shout, startled
when my stiff joints bend like birches,
my flat frame strides. If deadened longing
is revived, the body follows eager as a dog.

23

The Paralyzed Man

(MARK 2 : 1 – 12)

Those who have felt paralyzed know that it isn't a condition confined to the body. Depression can turn our limbs to dead weights; loveless relationships or dead-end jobs can pin us to the pallet; scar tissue can grow so tightly across the soul it smothers the spirit. Those suffering this affliction wonder if it will ever again be possible to jump out of bed with enthusiasm and walk confidently into the security of an inner home. Even if we know that healing lies within the hands of Jesus, we are powerless to go toward him. We know that all we need to do is push his door open a notch, but we don't have the strength to make the move. We can fully identify with Martin Marty's agony, "Why, when the cry is most intense, is the silence most stunning?"[75]

When we are in exile, it doesn't help to hear that Jesus "was at home" (Mark 2:1). The phrase suggests his security, clarity, integrity: all qualities that we sadly lack. John Shea points to a further irony: "in the gospels 'house' is often code for the church," the place where Jesus should be found. Yet here's the predicament: the church gathering creates such a crowd, it blocks access to Jesus. Where it should clear a path to him, it instead bars the paralyzed.[76]

It's heartening that not even the church can hinder access to Jesus when individuals seek him on behalf of their friend. So sometimes when we are paralyzed, the people of God "carry" us. Perhaps unconsciously, their prayers lift us up, their good actions continue, their kindness remains steadfast when we are incapable of prayer, of action, or of kindness. Most important for this story, they are innovative. If the door is blocked, they try the roof. The moral seems obvious: if the church impedes one path to Jesus, find another!

No obstacle can ever prevent his coming to the one who needs him. Just as Jesus saw the true identity of the bent woman, so he sees the child of God imprisoned by paralysis. He also sees the faith of the friends, an encouraging sign to those too weary to initiate their own healing, who must rely on the intervention of others.

As in the story of the bent woman, the sharp intrusion of the religious authorities introduces the negative to a scene that should be filled with awe and gratitude. The scribes place themselves in judgment over Jesus' compassion as though they could regulate the divine care. When everyone else rejoices in the cure, all they can do is fret. They cannot recognize miracle when they suspect a threat to their authority. In our day as well, officials cling to their tired authority, squandering it on inconsequentials while often overlooking human need.

Lest we get too simplistic about blaming officials, the passage also leads us to consider what blockades we erect to bar God; what obstacles we place on our path to Jesus; whether at times we have preferred a cozy inertia to the hard work of service. On a more positive note, it helps us appreciate the friends who at various times have borne our pallet when we were paralyzed, bringing us closer to healing.

Your turn:

- How do we at times create paralysis and erect blockades, denying that any good could come through groups or individuals we've dismissed?

- When you have felt paralyzed either in body or in spirit, what friends have carried you forward, bearing you toward healing?

24

Coming Together Creatively
MARK

Mark recently resigned a high position within the Catholic Church to take one in a brand new field. Despite a doctorate in theology and many years of experience in the church, he has found authentic witness in other places. While feeling some sadness about the time and energy invested in his first profession, he says, "There's a beauty to the study of theology, yet it can be perverse. Like pornography, bad theology can imprison, corrupt, and corrode. As Rabbi Friedman says in *Generation to Generation,* when an institution tries to control more and more, building walls higher and higher, the best and brightest escape. They move to environments where their talents are welcome and their gifts are honored." He could almost be speaking of someone imprisoned by paralysis, who finds the door impassable, but enters through the roof.

The Scribes Live On

Mark also addresses the problem of today's "scribes," the church officials: "How does one group of mostly elderly, white males have a privileged experience of the Spirit, authoritative for everyone else? They try to impose teachings and obligations on everyone that are often poorly thought out. The 'prince of the church' model begun in Europe to give the clergy status no longer works here. It's impossible to impose a dictatorship on a democracy. How can we believe that a great and good God is restricted to so few? When the self-righteousness is piled that high and the rug is eventually pulled from beneath it, then it's a long fall.

"The institutional church is certainly behaving as if it's in the death throes. When you're afraid, how do you act? You puff yourself up, shout louder, and hurt a lot of people. These actions betray the credibility of the Christ. If this is supposed to be Christ enfleshed, is it a faithful rendition? As an icon, the institution makes people have difficulty believing in God.

"So many people who stay in the institution waste a lot of energy on how to play the game: what to reveal, what not to reveal to officials. Those who work with the church keep believing it will deliver on its promises; then when it doesn't, we're shocked."

Mark speaks with admiration of one exception, a fellow theologian who stays in a church environment despite terrible oppression. Church authorities have condemned his book although they haven't read it; they have created innuendos against him which they will not state publicly. Why does he stay? The theologian explains his choice: "It has nothing to do with religion. It has everything to do with spirituality."

To place such an insight in perspective, it helps to remember that formal religion has flourished for only five percent of humanity's time on earth. In the West, it seems to be in decline, but "the revitalization and rediscovery of spirituality engages the human heart and imagination in a range of new and exciting ways."[77]

A Personal Sadness

Mark has discovered that excitement and creativity in his new job, as well as in his personal relationship with Daniel. On their right hands, they both wear beautiful interwoven circles of gold. When asked, Mark must fudge an answer to all but a few people he trusts: "I wear it on my right hand because I'm not married," he'll explain. "It was given to me by a dear friend."

But to the few with whom he feels safe, Mark will speak the truth: "I'm proud of my love for Daniel. Why can't I tell everyone how we exchanged these rings in commitment and have lived together for many happy years?" Clearly it saddens Mark that his primary relationship must be hidden in any circumstance related to the church. Yet, as if telling his own version of the friends who brought the paralytic, he says: "The only way we come to God is together. As the institutional dimension gets louder and more oppressive, it helps to remember that. When we get past that dimension, we can see how many people are really affiliated in spirit."

Lament of the Unpaid Mourner

It takes skill to pump the crowd, get a good
wail going, raise the usual hysteria.
I'm the best in the business — not to brag —
some call me before the corpse is cold.

But that day took me by surprise.
A child, it was, an easy melancholy.
When the flutes faltered, I knew
something was wrong. Before I could stop him

Someone silenced my best boys, my loudest widows.
One half-moan choked and hung, stillborn on the
silence — like my fist, clenched on the empty air.
"What's this?" I growled. "I need to make a living!"

He didn't give a fig. "Get her something to eat,"
I overheard. Where that girl was going, no one packs lunch.
But shrouds that should stay still as marble rumpled;
only warm contours and a shadowy hollow remained.

The best I could get might be a tip,
Jairus's grateful impulse to the wrong guy.
The bill expires when a dark kingdom slinks
away, driven by the pulse in a child's wrist.

25

The Dead Child

(M A R K   5 : 2 1 – 4 3)

In the voice of the unpaid mourner, we can recognize a sad, unredeemed part of ourselves. "Cut the hooey, hallucination, hoopla," we whine. We're resigned to a comfy lethargy, a sleepy sensibility. Our puny affairs roll along, quiet and mindless. We're busy enough with the numb routine, the relief of anesthesia, so we wave away intrusion. "Don't stir up large, ridiculous expectations. Don't wake the dead. The ideal, the joy, the energy that once coursed through our veins are better banished; we're wisely cynical now.

"Keep the deity distant, up in heaven, not mucking around in our business. God should be aloof and detached, not drinking our wine, talking to shady women, awakening a girl who's already gone. This religious stuff belongs in the temple, not sneaking into our homes, leaking into our markets, stirring up the dust of our streets. Start that kind of craziness and you never know where it will end — it's a pernicious plot to unnerve us and recruit our kids. We've grown accustomed to the persistent ache; leave us alone with the devil we know. Keep your wild, outrageous dreams, your surges of life."

Our attitudes are summarized by one searing line of Mark's gospel. When Jesus comes to the home of Jairus, he finds commotion: "people weeping and wailing loudly." To this scene, he tries to restore peace, harmony, and hope. He promises the people that the child is not dead, but asleep. Their reaction? *"...they laughed at him"* (Mark 5:40). We squirm uncomfortably with the resonance, for we too have sneered, thought new life impossible, been convinced that death had the final word.

All Jesus can do in the face of such indifference is "put them outside," banishing those that thrive off the culture of death. Only a small circle gathered in love can witness miracle: the mother and father, three faithful disciples. What they see is the simplest of gestures: he takes her by the hand. What they hear is gentle invitation, "Little girl, get up."

Buried in our hurts, nursing our wounds in safety, sometimes the last thing we want is the touch that brings us to life. We avoid the eye contact, the truth-telling, the music or beauty that touches the sensitive places. Still Jesus comes, to destabilize pious consolations, create reversals, and wreck havoc with our comfort zones. He comes especially to those who are invisible, ciphers even to themselves. With their longings numbed or deadened, they have been subservient too long. They have become the victims described by the poet Yeats,

> Too long a sacrifice
> Can make a stone of the heart.[78]

When Jesus touches the dead body of Jairus's daughter, the action makes him unclean by Jewish law. He cares little for the silliness of the rule, dismisses the taboo as miniscule in the face of the overwhelming need. We can almost imagine him brushing aside the constraints of our day, with which authorities attempt to curtail his power. Again he insists that his resurrection triumph, this time in us.

Your turn:

- Recall a time when hope seemed dead and life was restored.

- To what dead places in ourselves do we need Jesus to come now?

- What dreams pulsing with hope have we buried? What doors have we locked? To what rooms, within or without, have we vowed we'll never return?

- What inner or outer voices of wailing and commotion need to be cast aside so Jesus can enter our homes, our selves?

26

Terminal Diagnosis

L U K E

Luke had been a Catholic priest for twenty-five years, but now he calls his resignation from the priesthood "early retirement." "I like that PC term!" he laughs in retrospect, five years after leaving the active ministry. Deep concern for a church which he fears critically sick fills his conversation. Whatever his "official" status, Luke remains a priestly person.

Spirituality Drain

"Our number one problem is the spirituality drain. People aren't finding spirituality in the church; it's not personally or communally satisfying there. They're seeking this enrichment from other sources. It's sad because there's so much rich spirituality in the Catholic Church! Yet look at the best sellers — Deepak Chopra's and Thomas More's books, *Simple Abundance*. Much of the self-esteem literature talks about meditation and living simply. Books on money talk about detachment from it, yet too often, that's all people hear about at church!

"The spirituality drain is subtly undermining the church because people aren't being fed there. Parishes do their annual census, counting the attendees on holidays or on a designated date. Yet even though the Catholic population is up, attendance is down. Expectations are so low that people simply go out of a sense of obligation. I'm sure there are exceptions, and some personality types are happy with doing their duty.

"A couple years ago, tremendous moral issues had surfaced, like the oppression of the poor, weapons proliferation, and people's own emptiness. Yet the bishops' conference talked about reinstating meatless Fridays. How pitiable — such narrow thinking — in the face of all the world issues!"

Lack of Leadership

"The second problem I see is the lack of leadership from bishops and priests. The official church is no longer serving people, but serving itself. It's a human organization, and a human organization will preserve itself, like the survival of the species. The problem with ecclesiastical culture is that people don't even know it's there. It's a Zen-like dilemma: how do you help a fish discover water? How do you help leaders recognize a culture that's brought them to leadership, but is out of sync with the lives of most people?

"By culture, I mean a way of seeing the world and living our lives that isn't questioned. In the book *Mr. God, This Is Anna*, the little girl who's almost mystical can't wait to go to Sunday school. But after a few sessions, she doesn't want to return. Her guardian, surprised, asks why. Anna replies, 'The teacher makes God too small.'

"That's why people have little hope in organized religion. The church often has a fortress mentality; it's not the church helping the world, but the church defending itself. Fifty years ago, priests were the most educated people in the parish or town. That's no longer true. Lots of people have more expertise and education, especially in organization and administration, where many priests have shortcomings. It reminds me of what John Gardiner writes in *Grendal:* 'There is no conviction in the old priests' songs. There is only showmanship. No one in the kingdom is convinced that the gods have life in them. The weak observe the rites, taking their hats off, putting them on again, raising their arms. They press their palms together. But no one harbors unreasonable expectations.'

"People don't expect much from church leadership, which has become divisive and political. Leaders seem more interested in getting their personal agendas across than in meeting people's needs. I remember a theme from the '70s, that unity isn't uniformity, but there can be unity in plurality. You need all different instruments to perform a symphony work. In the church now, it's all one instrument, like a symphony played with violins alone.

"Furthermore, there's a lack of accountability for the jobs people do. I go to Sunday Mass, where I'm not spiritually nourished by the homily. I get some satisfaction from contact with the people. But basically it's not the shepherd serving the sheep; it's the sheep serving the shepherd. Loyal older Catholics step in and do the work the priest would normally take on his own shoulders.

"The problem isn't the amount of work priests have; it's the unrealistic expectations. They're supposed to be administrators, preachers, counselors, writers, consolers of the dying. Most aren't good managers because they've never had the training or supervision in the field. In the seminaries they're getting the same education they did in the '50s, before Vatican Council II. Most are taught to be teachers, defenders of faith, experts in canon law and liturgy. But it's so impractical; many have no experience leading prayer until they're deacons. By then it's too late — they're almost ordained. Some seminaries are trying to make advances, but for most the training is simply socialization into the clerical culture, new wine in old wine skins.

"Here's an example: recently a Midwestern bishop encouraged his priests to learn team leadership and skills. Yet at the end of their training, he sabotaged the whole process by saying, 'Remember: there's only one chair in my office!' He meant that only one person is accountable. No wonder morale is low among priests!"

Failure to Recognize the Baptized

"The third problem is our failure to honor the baptism of the laity. In that area, I see a real gap between theology and practice. People are baptized 'priest, prophet, and king' in God's reign, but that dignity is still not recognized in the church. We need to encourage top-notch people, train them, give them the theological background. Many retired lawyers would be better at processing annulments than some parish priests. They already have good legal minds and simply need a six-week course on marriage law. But the case load takes up a lot of priests' time.

"That's what I mean about the expectations crushing priests when laity do the job better. If a priest is good at visiting the sick, that's what he should do. Someone else can preach, unless the priest is the best homilist in the parish. It has to do with talent, not hours of study. It depends on personal gifts and some just don't have the gift of preaching.

"When I go to a priests' meeting, I see few who look healthy. They're not necessarily sick, but they look tired, depressed, often overweight. I recently went out to dinner with a priest in his thirties. He was saying five Masses a weekend and holding four parish council meetings in a week. He looked so exhausted, I thought it was going to be the last supper!

"In terms of the laity, we must focus more on adult education. Not that we don't educate children, but that we recognize learning is a life-long process. Most people quit studying theology or spirituality in eighth grade or high school and that's where they've stayed. An objection might be that if they go to Mass, they're educated by the homily. But most people aren't getting anything from the homilies. Some priests have good style, but no substance, just a few cute jokes.

"We're told to pray for vocations to priesthood and religious life. In our diocese we have an annual march of sixteen miles for vocations. But we've got to look at people's baptismal vocations instead. When bishops insist on praying for vocations to the ordained priesthood, they have no appreciation for the priesthood of the laity. They've prayed for thirty years and the message is clear: God is saying *no*.

"One of my professors once said, 'The church is the only human organization that kills its own soldiers,' referring to priests and religious. The American bishops should start acting like the bishops Vatican II promised us. They are still prisoners of the Vatican, so they hold American Catholics captive too. Again, our wonderful documents, guidelines, and books aren't consistent with practice.

"Many priests who've left active ministry have gotten married. But if their life had been fulfilled, if priestly life was really all it's cracked up to be, they would still be in. They left to survive. Maybe it took a woman to help them see how enjoyable life could be. Few of those who have left are ever shown appreciation, nor are their talents used. Big mistake!"

While Luke may not be shown official appreciation, it comes from the migrants he ministers to, his friends and co-workers. He has found health outside the church and his personal dance continues.

Your turn:

- Choose one character who asked healing from Jesus: the leper (Mark 1:40), the paralytic (Mark 2:3), the woman with a hemorrhage (Matt. 9:19–21), the woman bent double (Luke 13:10–11), the blind man (Mark 10:51), or the dead child (Mark 5:22–23). Think about why you identify with that person and imagine a similar condition in yourself, although it may not be physical.

- Then visualize Jesus coming to cure you. Conclude by continuing the reading: for the leper, Mark 1:41; for the paralytic, Mark 2:11; for the woman with a hemorrhage, Matt. 9:22; for the woman bent double, Luke 13:12–13; for the blind man, Mark 10:52; for the dead child, Mark 5:41–42. How do you feel as you read the words of healing?

- If you could talk further with Barb, Mark, and Luke, what would you like to ask them or say to them?

– Part V –

Partners in the Dance

If our civilization is to be saved — if *we* are to be saved, it will not be by Romans but by saints.
— THOMAS CAHILL, *How the Irish Saved Civilization*

In a snowy scene at a retreat house, a woman stood at the foot of a hulking, wooden cross. Her red jacket and purple pants contrasted with the snow surrounding her; her face was turned away. An anonymous figure, she was in many ways symbolic. She was not simply "standing at the foot of the cross" as Christians have done for centuries. She was holding tightly to its base, her face pressed against its rough wood in evocative silhouette.

A passerby could only speculate about what she suffered: whether it was great and tragic loss, or the small, ongoing pains that eke away the energies and drain the spirit. Against a backdrop of granite mountains, she was soft and vulnerable, a frail human form. She symbolized not only those who suffer, but those who know where to bring their pain. The symbol of all suffering holds the hope of all salvation.

To seek suffering for its own sake is dysfunctional. Enough pain enters everyone's life unsought. But to seek an understanding of pain in the cross of Christ has helped people for many years. Christians come to the cross not to seek suffering, but to find Christ. At all times and in all situations, he is our center and hope.

When we get caught up in struggle among church factions, it is wise to remember advice once given to the Corinthian community: "...each of you says, 'I belong to Paul,' or I belong to Apollos,' or 'I belong to Cephas,' or 'I belong to Christ.' Has Christ been divided? Was Paul crucified for you?" (1 Cor. 1:12–13) When Thomas Cahill speaks of the saints in the quote above, he means those who have rooted their life in Christ, as opposed to the Romans obsessed with power, authority, law and order.

Those who recognize the silliness of church divisions, like some of the people profiled in this book, have sought an alternate way, a stronger tradition, a less restricted spirituality. Always conscious of their own imperfections, they have chosen to live the gospel rather than please the authorities. They have opted to love the battered face of Christ more than ecclesial power. They guide us to sources of nurture that have helped them survive the struggle with fortitude and humor. Above all, they invite us to keep the dance flowing gracefully. Wherever the music plays and the dance begins, it echoes the cosmic dance, in which we partner with God, the saints, and each other. More about that company in this final section, which includes a reflection on identifying with Jesus' passion, a profile of Alison, and a meditation on Mary Magdalene.

Mary Magdalene
in the Dawn Garden
(J O H N   2 0 : 1 – 1 8)

Only after the men tromp busily away,
their thorough investigation complete,
does feathery wing flutter in the tomb.
Only to her stubborn tears do angels speak,
asking in the cool shadow the question
he would repeat in garden sunlight:
"Woman, why do you weep?"

Cutting to the core, not interested
in her awards or medals, not much
concerned about her joys: he comes
to the sad, lost, hidden places.
Sleepless, she bumbles to the
second question: "Whom do you seek?"
As if he didn't know the answer.

He asks as kind reminder
that she looks not for security
or applause or grace, but
for one dear, camouflaged face.
The stab of "sir" in her reply, formal,
still blind, not recognizing him
who had been close as her own skin.

She volunteers, of course, for the impossible.
"I'll drag the heavy corpse — just tell
me where it is!" Wrapped in her name, memory and
recognition, silencing sorrow. The bell of
clear response, his name in turn. She must
fly, instinctive, to hold him, defying death,
arms circling broken bones that hum with life.

27

Identifying with Jesus' Passion

Reflection

Imagine a dear friend, someone you can really confide in. You have talked before — indeed, you have made some major decisions and have had some deep insights through conversations with this friend. Even if time or space separates you, you begin easily where you left off. You share important values and similar senses of humor; you like the same things. This friend is familiar with your background, your work, your family. He or she fits into your experience almost as comfortably as you do and does not need elaborate explanations.

What does this person look like? sound like? What is one of your favorite memories of a time together?...

Now imagine sharing one of your favorite settings — the corner table at the Italian restaurant, a field of wildflowers, a lakeside cabin. What do you see there? hear? smell? touch? taste?...

Imagine that you and your friend are together in this place, to talk about your current struggles. What do you say to your friend? What does your friend say to you?

Now a third person joins your conversation. Everything we know of friendship prepares us for his entrance. For this person is Jesus, who said, "I do not call you servants. I call you friends." Imagine him sitting down with you, walking beside you, or taking you in his arms. Tell him what's on your mind. If you find it hard to begin, pray these words from Nestor of Magydus:

> *With my Christ I have ever been,*
> *With my Christ, I am now,*
> *With my Christ, I will be forever....*[79]

Let the words wash over you repeatedly as a reminder that Christ is with you in this as he has been with you in every other crisis and joy of your life. He does not offer magic answers, but he brings the rich assurance of his constant presence.

As you listen quietly for his response, you can count on his compassionate courtesy. He will not say any of the things that well-meaning people sometimes say inadvertently, which only twist the knife in the wound. You will not hear,

- *"I saw it coming, but I didn't want to worry you."*

- *"Well, if I were you, I would've gotten out of that situation a long time ago."*

- *"But there must be some good reason this happened!"*

What you hear may sound more like this: "I am so sorry. I know how much time and energy and care you poured into that job (or relationship, or community). You must feel like all your efforts have vanished down a black hole. Are you angry? bitter? Have you lost your anchor or self-confidence? Are you feeling rejected, humiliated, unappreciated, ashamed? I understand. I lost everything once."

•

Jesus was betrayed by everything he had every right to expect from his religion. The turncoats were, after all, not the Roman occupying authorities, but the chief priests, annoyed by the raising of Lazarus. They decided that if they didn't stop such miraculous signs, everyone would believe in him. Their logic may be askew, but such arguments have always been contorted. Somehow, they reasoned, if the people followed Jesus, the Romans would destroy the temple and the nation. "So from that day on they planned to put him to death" (John 11:53). They put out orders like a sinister net: anyone seeing him at the religious celebration of Passover should inform on him. Like contemporary authorities who place *everyone* under suspicion, the chief priests decide to kill Lazarus as well (as if they could undo the astonishing raising from the tomb, or murder the resurrected one).

After striking a deal with religious authorities, Judas the traitor led to the garden "a detachment of guards sent by the chief priests and the Pharisees, all with lanterns and torches and weapons" (John 18:3). After Jesus is pushed like a puppet between the high priests Annas and Caiaphas, he is sent to the Roman governor Pilate, who tries to evade involvement in the case. Pilate protests that it seems to be an internal struggle: "Take him yourselves, and try him by your own law" (John 18:31). Pilate's words to Jesus painfully underscored the betrayal by his own: "Am I a Jew? It is your own people and the chief priests who have handed you over to me" (John 18:35).

Relentlessly, the chief priests incite the crowds to demand the release of Barabbas the brigand. When Pilate, the voice of secular power, finds no case against Jesus, the chief priests shout, "Crucify him!" (John 19:6). In stunning self-condemnation, the highest ranking members of the religious caste vow allegiance not to God, but to the occupying power: "We have no king except Caesar" (John 19:16). We may be appalled by contemporary collusions between church and corrupt governments; this one set the precedent.

The chief priests must have felt enormous relief after the crucifixion. There had been another skirmish with Pilate over the wording of the notice on the cross, when he finally revealed his utter exasperation with the priests. But, by and large, they had done the job they had to do. Of course it wasn't pleasant, but they had to defend the people from this upstart. They had only carried out their responsibility, prescribed by the law. It was unfortunate, but now it was over. They could get back to the Torah and temple, conducting worship and "business as usual."

And Jesus had proven for all time his solidarity with those who suffer. As one commentator writes:

> In this chosen solidarity Christ lets their poverty get to him, become his cause, become part of his felt identity, as he struggles to bring them to the realization that God's reign is offered to them as a gracious empowerment of their lives. The suffering which he chose during the course of his life consisted in sharing the life of those suffering not only from physical and mental ailments, but also from the oppressive

structures of their day: *the elitism of urban (Jerusalem) religion*, the destructive division of the country into *religious* and economic "haves" and "have nots."[80] (Emphasis added.)

But let's get back to you.

In the story of Jesus' ordeal, did any of the words ring with special poignancy? the tortured logic used to plot the arrest? the traitor? the role of the priests in his betrayal? the kiss?

Now that you are going through your own particular struggle, does it increase your solidarity with Jesus in his passion, or with others who suffer throughout the world?

If you have lost a job, are there other areas of life and growth which ground you — your family, your home, your other interests? If you cherish them, does it make the loss more bearable?

If you have lost a relationship or community, where else could you look for some of the things it gave you: challenge, stimulation, rest, security, sympathy, commonality, an "anchor"?

If you have lost your professional or creative outlet, where else might you channel those energies?

If a door has closed, you are right to grieve its closing. Take all the time you need. But then, when you are ready, start looking around. What other doors might be opening? Where else might God be leading you next? Could some fruitful seeds be buried in this wintry earth?

Remember an experience from your past when an event which seemed horrific actually led to some good happenings. Savor those memories, because it is always possible that the crisis you are going through now could also contain a hidden treasure.

You may wish to end as you began, by repeating the prayer of Nestor, or saying this one from the Celtic tradition:

> *I am serene because I know thou lovest me.*
> *Because thou lovest me,*
> *nought can move me from my peace.*
> *Because thou lovest me,*
> *I am one to whom all good has come.*[81]

Your turn:

- If you were to talk now with someone struggling with the church, would your advice be affected by anything you read here? Why or why not?

- What final words do you want to say to Jesus? What might he say to you?

28

Loss and New Life

A L I S O N

A pattern of loss and gain has alternated throughout Alison's life. It is not hard to imagine her waiting expectantly at the tomb; she is the bearer of that hope that Václav Havel distinguished from optimism: "[Hope] is not the conviction that something will turn out well, but the certainty that something makes sense regardless of how it turns out. It is hope, above all, which gives us the strength to live and continually try new things."

A grandmother and spiritual director who holds a master's degree in religion, Alison has been involved in enough church reform projects to exhaust the ordinary mortal. Currently she contends with a perennial problem: the death of a wonderful pastor and friend, the installation of an incompetent pastor. Yet she struggles from a faithful stance. Talking to her reveals how faith in different forms has always been an important part of her life.

A Constant Faith

"I grew up in a small town with no churches. My dad was Mormon, but he managed to put seven children through nearby Catholic schools. In those days, we Catholic kids couldn't even go to Mrs. Logan's hymn sing! I guess they were afraid of exposing us to other Christian traditions. But I knew, despite what everyone said, that my wonderful non-Catholic relatives were in heaven alongside the Catholic ones.

"When it came time to choose a graduate school, I wanted to broaden my concept of Christianity, not narrow it. I might become rigid at a Catholic school, and I didn't want that to happen. So I went to a Methodist university. One of the professors warned me at the outset, 'Don't let us take your faith away.' If anything, my education in an ecumenical setting solidified my Catholicism!

"I realized how much we have, even though at times it was painful sitting next to women who had the choice to say, 'I want to be ordained or lay,' a choice we didn't have. My husband offered: 'If you want to be a priest, we'll just become Episcopalian.'

"I turned him down. I've been to many ecumenical services and worked on ecumenical staffs, but something about being Catholic is etched on my soul. It might get blurry or get rubbed over, but it can't be eradicated."

Alison is steadfast; she too would wait with blurred vision and talk to a gardener she did not recognize. Asked why she remains in her faith tradition, she replies, "I took seriously the proclamation of Vatican Council II that we the people are the church. Ordained persons constitute only 1 percent, a figure I learned in Rome, at the alternate synod on the laity. What keeps me going back are the friends who keep working at it day in and out because they know the church can be better."

Call to Reform

"It's not making a new law or issuing a new edict that will do it; our acting out of what Christ calls us to creates reform. It helps to go to people with listening ears, who encourage me to stay where I am, as they stay where they are.

"We certainly wouldn't stay in our parish because of the pastor! For starters, the guy has no social graces. We've been in a dinner group with him and have been appalled when he has told a host or hostess to leave the party, run to the liquor store, and buy *his* brand of booze. When everyone brings food to a potluck, he'll complain about the broccoli: 'That is the most god-awful vegetable. Gives me gas!' What a total lack of sensitivity to the people who have put time into cooking and entertaining!

"Everyone else kowtows and calls him Father Miller. I call him Sam. He still doesn't know my name, and we've eaten dinner to-gether three times. I'm the only parish member in a wheelchair, but he still doesn't notice. It reminds me of the time I was in a discussion group with the archbishop for several years. When he asked if we had any questions, I pointed at our name tags and said, 'If we're supposed to be so friendly, why do you still call me Alison, and I still call you Archbishop Dunn?'

"Our pastor makes grating remarks from the altar that have nothing to do with what's going on. At his formal installation, after someone else talked about what it means to be pastor, he didn't thank us or say it was good to be here. He stood at the altar and bellowed, 'Well, you're stuck with me now!' It completely blew the dignity of the occasion.

"But as a woman and a lay person, I don't relish giving the power of my spirituality over to the hierarchy or the clergy. I refuse to let someone else keep me in or out of a church based on what he did. My spirituality rests with God, not with some priest. It would give him a false sense of power and make me feel less than God intended me to be. We left one parish because of the priest, and we won't do that again. It meant leaving too many friends behind. So we go to the Jesuit retreat house once a month and get our 'fix' of good liturgy and a good homily."

Model and Mentor

"This situation with the pastor is surely harder because we've recently lost a wonderful pastor and friend. Bob, who died last year, related to people as persons, not just 'one of my flock,' cared about all aspects of people's lives, and was extremely accepting of wherever a person was. I still remember his homily on divorce, when he said how sad it was that people were forced out of the church because of marital status. Jesus says to everyone, 'Come, you are mine.' That includes *everyone*, whether an institutional rule has been broken or not. That person is still loved by God. I can't imagine Jesus or Bob saying, 'Everyone come to my table except you, because you've been divorced.' The people gave him a standing ovation that day!

"Bob had a personal dignity and he treated the church with dignity. Sure, he could laugh about the institution and tell funny jokes about it, but he still had that respect. As a people, we need ritual and symbol. Those symbols are deeply rooted in the psyche. When Bob lifted the chalice, you knew it meant something to him. And because it meant so much to him, it meant something to us.

"The church we sometimes labor under now isn't necessarily the church that was born out of the gospel. We've gotten so far away from that. Some of us stay in, not hoping someone else will do it, but that together we'll have the strength to make it more of what Jesus intended. I don't worry much about laws made by celibate men wearing skirts in Rome — many of them have nothing to do with me.

"Another admirable thing about Bob was his friendship with Megan, a mutual friend and a vowed religious. Priests who have had an important woman in their lives are different, more sensitive and respectful. The unknown frightens us, and they aren't frightened. But a man who doesn't have women friends has an almost adolescent curiosity or defensiveness. 'This is an unknown quantity,' he says, 'so I protect myself by pushing it away, becoming defensive about it.' Some of the priests are so worried, they're afraid to enter into friendship with a woman. She's the 'temptress' who might endanger his vocation. Megan got a beautiful card after Bob's funeral from someone who said she'd learned so much from them about what a male-female friendship could be.

"I've also learned a lot from splendid mentors. It feels important to me to say I'm a Catholic. I don't want to learn new symbols, can't imagine myself filling in forms with anything but 'Catholic' under 'denomination,' even though it frustrates the daylights out of me. I even get annoyed when people say 'I'm a *recovering* Catholic.' I respect each person's right to find their own religious path, but don't denigrate the church with a cutesy saying!

"A friend of mine in seminary left the Catholic Church to become a Methodist minister. It made me terribly sad to hear of her struggles, although she made the only right choice for her. We lose so many good people that way! Married priests, the women who truly have a gift: they'd make marvelous ordained people, so it's a great sadness."

The Power Within

"Many of the people I care about are involved in creating new rituals. I'm not against it, but I don't feel that same drivenness to come up with something different. I like the Eucharist; it doesn't bother me that it's male-dominated. The fact that it's a man on the altar doesn't interfere with my ability to worship. I'm not there to worship the man; I'm there to glorify God and be in communion with the people. The priest is a part of that, but not all of it. So I can live with some 'hims'; although there are a few 'hims' I'd rather see than others!

"I want to be part of what makes the good happen. I want to stay in what means the most to me, or I would've left years ago. I'm not going to let it slide any more than I'd quit correcting my kids' little mistakes. I want to be there to be an influence on it.

"In the heyday after Vatican II, Bob was my mentor and friend. He believed its teachings to his core, and planted them in me at a deep level. Maybe what we can model to our kids is steadiness. We don't just keep hoping for something better; we work to bring it about."

The ancient themes of death and resurrection come alive again in Alison's story. No wheelchair could ever keep her from dancing.

29

Identifying with Mary Magdalene

To those who have had intense struggles with the church or have been deeply wounded in the fray, the symptoms sound familiar: utter emptiness, a loss of trust in life as a whole, God seeming absent or dead. This sense of paralysis is not unique: the first disciples also experienced it. In the nightmarish events of a few days, everything they had come to believe in, to count on, to value, vanished. They cast about futilely for something to take its place, perhaps knowing subconsciously, without admitting it, that nothing ever could. The void left by Jesus' death was too vast for anything or anyone else to ever fill. Their best, highest hopes froze. As they tell the stranger on the road to Emmaus: "But we had hoped that he was the one to redeem Israel" (Luke 24:21).

The Loss of God

Harsh reality demanded that they surrender this fond hope of redemption. They must also make a radical change in their image of God. For them, Jesus' presence on earth had introduced a new face of God. No longer distant and punitive, God became "Abba," close and compassionate. God dwelt not only in the mysterious clouds of Mt. Sinai, but as close as a shared meal, a hand brushing the forehead of a feverish woman, a thought-provoking story, a group of friends toying with a pun or wrestling with a question. Jesus taught that God's reign was *within;* people excluded from every perk, every social event, every temple ritual had suddenly become honored guests at a banquet where the host was divine.

Jesus' crucifixion meant losing all that. Their dream of God's reign was aborted; their hopes lay dead as puddles of blood drying in dust or a corpse wrapped in linen, laid in a cave. Brian McDermott describes their loss:

> They had experienced in Christ not a God of guilt, of distance and threat to the rebellious ego, but the "new God" of loving nearness and a shocking kind of mercy. Christ's crucifixion cut off at the quick this unprecedented experience. *This* God dies in their eyes and shows up as *powerless,* completely powerless, because the death of Christ has the power to render this God dead for them.... Christ encountered the disciples on a most profound level where their deepest identity was at stake, the level in them where their trust or mistrust about life *as a whole* was played out. This level is the place where we are utterly empty if deprived of the experience of God and the place filled with life when God is near.[82]

We are so accustomed to having God's grace mediated, through friends or family, through nature, the sacraments, or the worship life of the church, that we rarely fall back on God's grace alone. When we do it's a difficult passage into the dark night of the soul. It's the agony in the garden, the anguished, lonely cry from the cross, "My God, why have you forsaken me?"

"Why Are You Weeping?"

Perhaps one of the starkest portraits of this abandoned state is that of Mary Magdalene outside the tomb: alone, weeping, confused, disoriented. If we recognize something of ourselves in her, or have known the seeming futility of her vigil there, then we can sense a little of the emptiness she must feel. Jesus' first question to her touches this hollow within: "Woman, why do you weep?"

It's a question worth asking ourselves regularly. The Christian tradition has always honored the place of suffering as the place of growth. If we ask ourselves Jesus' question, we may find that, at least on the surface, things seem to be going fairly well. If we look deeper, we may find the alienation from church, the failed relationship, the injustice of ... Soon we discover that our initial response only skimmed the surface. We can become smug and shallow if we do not name and enter the sadnesses. Apparently they are as important to Jesus as any award or honor. Furthermore, they give us a wedge of understanding all the people who suffer far more than we do.

It would have been natural for Jesus to trumpet his victory. "Look, Mary! I conquered death!" Such a story is told by a priest who visited a first grade classroom the day after Easter. "What were Jesus' first words after the resurrection?" he asked the children. Most looked blank, but one little girl waved her hand eagerly. "I know!" she called. "All right, Sonja, what were they?" She stood, thrust her arms skyward and proclaimed, "Tah Duh!" The story is charming, but it points up one fact: Jesus' first words had nothing to do with his own resurrection and everything to do with touching the sorrow in Mary's soul.

"Whom Are You Looking for?"

His second question, "Whom are you looking for?" seems to have an obvious answer. "You!" Mary might shout. "Why else would I be hanging around a tomb by myself in the darkness? Only the thought of you could bring me here." We could in turn ask ourselves: "Who is Christ for me in my present situation? Where do I look for him?"

We might also be searching for ourselves: perhaps a hidden part of the self, a part never integrated because of embarrassment or social constraints or other priorities. Or perhaps a wonderful part longs to come to birth, the part that sings or dances or can be wonderfully compassionate to others. There is usually more to ourselves than what we often see, the workhorse buried under a mountain of detail that we *must* complete each day. Prompted by Jesus' question to Mary, we might ask ourselves, "What part of ourselves do we want to befriend and bring forth?"

Only after the two questions that can prompt so much reflection does Jesus allow recognition, achieved by his calling Mary's name. She had lost all hope. Then suddenly, it was back. He was back.

If we feel within ourselves a void corresponding to Mary's, we can also have hope: that space can become sanctuary. The place of emptiness turns into the place of transcendence. There, without the usual mediations, God can fill the vacuum. "In the Easter appearances this man Christ stood, as it were, in that 'place' in the disciples where God alone can come and go. This particular person, totally human and totally God, gives himself to be experienced in that place of ultimate emptiness and longing which is our transcendence, our creatureliness, where only God...can be present."[83]

If the space within us feels desolate as a tomb, if the light has not yet dawned in the garden shadows, we are in good company. In such a place, Mary walked bewildered, and there she met the risen Christ. We who weep seek him too; tenderly he touches eyes blinded by tears.

Your turn:

- If you could continue the conversation with any of the actual people whose stories are told here (Laura, Maura, Belle, Jean, Paula, Julia, Cara, Scott, Barb, Mark, Luke, or Alison), whom would you choose? What would you say?

- If you could continue the conversation with one of the scriptural figures (the Canaanite woman, Thomas, the woman at the well, the fishermen at breakfast, the bent woman, the paralyzed man, the dead child, Mary Magdalene), whom would you choose? What would you say?

Notes

Introduction

1. Dorothy Day, *The Long Loneliness* (New York: HarperSan-Francisco, 1997), 179.

2. Richard Rohr with John Bookser Feister, *Jesus' Plan for a New World* (Cincinnati: St. Anthony Messenger Press, 1996), 8.

3. Robert Barron, "You're Holier Than You Know," *U.S. Catholic*, October 1998, 11.

4. Gail Ramshaw, *Words around the Table* (Chicago: Liturgy Training Publications, 1991), 56.

1. Why Dance?

5. Quoted in Anne Lamott, *Traveling Mercies* (New York: Pantheon, 1999), 86.

6. Robert Barron, *And Now I See . . . : A Theology of Transformation* (New York: Crossroad, 1998), 152.

7. Joyce Rupp, *May I Have this Dance?* (Notre Dame, Ind.: Ave Maria Press, 1992), 13.

8. Diarmuid O'Murchu, *Quantum Theology* (New York: Crossroad, 1997), 41.

9. Quoted in Sam Keen, *To a Dancing God* (New York: Harper and Row, 1970), 51.

10. O'Murchu, *Quantum Theology*, 41.

11. Ibid., 42.

12. For more of this interpretation of Abraham and Sarah's story, see Sara Maitland, *Angel and Me* (Harrisburg, Pa.: Morehouse Publishing, 1997), 3–35.

13. Frederick Buechner, *Peculiar Treasures* (New York: HarperSan-Francisco, 1979), 173.

14. Thomas Merton, *New Seeds of Contemplation* (New York: New Directions, 1972), 296–97.

15. O'Murchu, *Quantum Theology*, 47.

16. Ibid., 45.

17. Ibid., 40.

18. Ibid., 48.

19. Ibid., 80.

20. Quoted in Jeannette Batz, "Embodying Praise," *National Catholic Reporter*, Special Spirituality Section, December 4, 1998, 36.

2. Why Meditate?

21. John Shea, *Gospel Light* (New York: Crossroad, 1998), 110.
22. Ibid., 113.
23. Ibid., 158.

3. Why the Margins?

24. John Shea, *Gospel Light* (New York: Crossroad, 1998), 43.

5. From Question to Invitation: Thomas

25. Brian McDermott, "With Him, in Him: The Graces of the Spiritual Exercises," *Studies in the Spirituality of Jesuits* 18, no. 4 (September 1986): 24.
26. Bernard Häring, *My Witness of the Church*, quoted in Kathleen Cahalan, " 'Still Spiritually Alive': Remembering Bernard Häring," *America*, August 15, 1998, 14.
27. Brennan Hill, "Curran on Häring," Letter to the Editor, *National Catholic Reporter*, August 28, 1998, 18.

6. From Clergy to Art: Vincent van Gogh

28. Irving Stone, ed., *Dear Theo: The Autobiography of Vincent van Gogh* (Garden City, N.Y.: Doubleday, 1937), 15.
29. Ibid., 7.
30. Ibid., 40.
31. Ibid., 32.
32. Ibid., 43.
33. Ibid., 50.
34. Ibid., 46.
35. *The Complete Letters*, 531, III, 25, quoted in Megan McKenna, *Advent, Christmas, and Epiphany: Stories and Reflections on the Daily Readings* (Maryknoll, N.Y.: Orbis, 1998), 16.

7. From Exile to Torrent of Love: Mechthild of Magdeburg

36. Carol Lee Flinders, *Enduring Grace* (New York: HarperSanFrancisco, 1993), 75.
37. Ibid., 51.

38. Ibid.
39. Ibid., 56.

9. From Towering to Tiny: Belle

40. Alice Walker, *In Search of Our Mothers' Gardens* (San Diego: Harcourt Brace Jovanovich, 1983), 232.
41. Ibid., 241.
42. Wendy Beckett, *Sister Wendy's Book of Saints* (London: Dorling Kindersley, 1998), 91.

12. From Narrow to Broader Church

43. Tom Beaudoin, "Beginning Afresh: Gen-X Catholics," *America,* November 21, 1998, 12.
44. Tim Unsworth, "Young Catholics," Special Spirituality Section, *National Catholic Reporter,* December 4, 1998, 26.

Part III: Great Thirsts and High Hopes

45. June Jordan, "Poem for South African Women," quoted in Kathleen Fischer, *Women at the Well* (Mahwah, N.J.: Paulist Press, 1988), 84.

13. Great Desires

46. Brian McDermott, "With Him in Him: The Graces of the Spiritual Exercises," *Studies in the Spirituality of Jesuits* 18, no. 4 (September 1986): 23.
47. Catherine of Siena, *The Dialogue,* trans. Suzanne Noffke (New York: Paulist, 1980), 25.
48. E. Edward Kinerk, S.J., "Eliciting Great Desires: Their Place in the Spirituality of the Society of Jesus," *Studies in the Spirituality of Jesuits* 16, no. 5 (November 1984): 2.
49. Frank Houdek, *Guided by the Spirit* (Chicago: Loyola University Press, 1996), 77.
50. D. H. Lawrence, quoted in J. Robert Baker and others, eds., *A Baptism Sourcebook* (Chicago: Liturgy Training Publications, 1993), 162.
51. John Kavanaugh, S.J., *The Word Engaged* (Maryknoll, N.Y.: Orbis, 1997), 82.
52. Carol Lee Flinders, *Enduring Grace* (New York: HarperSanFrancisco, 1993), 56–67.
53. Ibid., 57.

54. For a brief and readable introduction, see William Barry, S.J., *God's Passionate Desire and Our Response* (Notre Dame, Ind.: Ave Maria Press, 1993).

55. Charles Frazier, *Cold Mountain* (New York: Atlantic Monthly Press, 1997), 334.

56. Patricia O'Connell Killen, *Finding Our Voices* (New York: Crossroad, 1997), 117.

57. Ibid., 45.

14. Deep Wells

58. Gail Ramshaw, *Words around the Table* (Chicago: Liturgy Training Publications, 1991), 18.

59. Ibid.

60. Patricia O'Connell Killen, *Finding Our Voices* (New York: Crossroad, 1997), 31.

61. Ibid., 29.

62. See Mary Belenky and others, *Women's Ways of Knowing* (New York: Basic Books, 1986).

63. Etty Hillesum, quoted in J. Robert Baker and others, eds., *A Baptism Sourcebook* (Chicago: Liturgy Training Publications, 1993), 64.

64. John Shea, *Gospel Light* (New York: Crossroad, 1998), 97.

65. O'Connell Killen, *Finding Our Voices,* 38.

66. Ibid., 34.

17. The Blue-Green Solace of Nature

67. Rumi, *The Essential Rumi,* trans. Coleman Barks with John Moyne (New York: HarperSanFrancisco, 1995), 280.

68. Robert Ellsberg, *All Saints* (New York: Crossroad, 1998), 27.

69. Melissa Nussbaum, *I Will Arise This Day* (Chicago: Liturgy Training Publications, 1996), 91, 95.

18. Charcoal Fires

70. Dom Helder Camara, *Through the Gospel with Dom Helder Camara* (Maryknoll, N.Y.: Orbis, 1986).

71. James Dunning, *Echoing God's Word* (Arlington, Va.: North American Forum on the Catechumenate, 1993), 304.

72. Helen Prejean, "A Way Out of No Way," *America,* August 29, 1998, 7.

73. Ibid.

74. Ibid., 8.

23. The Paralyzed Man

75. Martin Marty, *A Cry of Absence* (San Francisco: Harper & Row, 1983), 147.
76. John Shea, *Gospel Light* (New York: Crossroad, 1998), 117–18.

24. Coming Together Creatively: Mark

77. Diarmuid O'Murchu, *Quantum Theology* (New York: Crossroad, 1997), 42.

25. The Dead Child

78. William Butler Yeats, "Easter, 1916," in M. L. Rosenthal, ed., *Selected Poems and Two Plays of William Butler Yeats* (New York: Macmillan, 1962), 86.

27. Identifying with Jesus' Passion

79. Quoted in Melissa Nussbaum, *I Will Lie Down This Night* (Chicago: Liturgy Training Publications, 1995), 44.
80. Brian McDermott, "With Him, in Him: The Graces of the Spiritual Exercises," *Studies in the Spirituality of Jesuits* 18, no. 4 (September 1986): 14.
81. Quoted in Nussbaum, *I Will Lie Down This Night*, 94.

29. Identifying with Mary Magdalene

82. Brian McDermott, "With Him, in Him: The Graces of the Spiritual Exercises," *Studies in the Spirituality of Jesuits* 18, no. 4 (September 1986): 22–23.
83. Ibid., 24.

Bibliography

Baker, Robert, and others, eds. *A Baptism Sourcebook*. Chicago: Liturgy Training Publications, 1993.

Barron, Robert. "You're Holier Than You Know." *U.S. Catholic* (October 1998).

———*And Now I See...: A Theology of Transformation*. New York: Crossroad, 1998.

Barry, William, S.J. *God's Passionate Desire and Our Response*. Notre Dame, Ind.: Ave Maria Press, 1993.

Batz, Jeannette. "Embodying Praise." *National Catholic Reporter*. Special Spirituality Section (December 4, 1998).

Beaudoin, Tom. "Beginning Afresh: Gen-X Catholics." *America* (November 21, 1998).

Beckett, Wendy. *Sister Wendy's Book of Saints*. London: Dorling Kindersley, 1998.

Belenky, Mary, and others. *Women's Ways of Knowing*. New York: Basic Books, 1986.

Buechner, Frederick. *Peculiar Treasures*. New York: HarperSanFrancisco, 1979.

Camara, Dom Helder. *Through the Gospel with Dom Helder Camara*. Maryknoll, N.Y.: Orbis, 1986.

Catherine of Siena. *The Dialogue*. Trans. Suzanne Noffke. New York: Paulist, 1980.

cummings, e. e. *Poems, 1923–1954*. New York: Harcourt Brace & World, 1954.

Day, Dorothy. *The Long Loneliness*. New York: HarperSanFrancisco, 1997.

Dunning, James. *Echoing God's Word*. Arlington, Va.: North American Forum on the Catechumenate, 1993.

Ellsberg, Robert. *All Saints*. New York: Crossroad, 1998.

Fischer, Kathleen. *Women at the Well*. Mahwah, N.J.: Paulist Press, 1988.

———. *Enduring Grace*. New York: HarperSanFrancisco, 1993.

Frazier, Charles. *Cold Mountain*. New York: Atlantic Monthly Press, 1997.

Houdek, Frank. *Guided by the Spirit*. Chicago: Loyola University Press, 1996.

Kavanaugh, John, S.J. *The Word Engaged*. Maryknoll, N.Y.: Orbis, 1997.

Keen, Sam. *To a Dancing God*. New York: Harper and Row, 1970.

Kinerk, E. Edward, S.J. "Eliciting Great Desires: Their Place in the Spirituality of the Society of Jesus." *Studies in the Spirituality of Jesuits* 16, no. 5 (November 1984).

Lamott, Anne. *Traveling Mercies*. New York: Pantheon, 1999.

Maitland, Sara. *Angel and Me*. Harrisburg, Pa.: Morehouse Publishing, 1997.

Marty, Martin. *A Cry of Absence*. San Francisco: Harper & Row, 1983.

McDermott, Brian. "With Him, in Him: The Graces of the Spiritual Exercises." *Studies in the Spirituality of Jesuits* 18, no. 4 (September 1986).

McKenna, Megan. *Advent, Christmas, and Epiphany: Stories and Reflections on the Daily Readings*. Maryknoll, N.Y.: Orbis, 1998.

Merton, Thomas. *New Seeds of Contemplation*. New York: New Directions, 1972.

Nussbaum, Melissa. *I Will Arise This Day*. Chicago: Liturgy Training Publications, 1996.

———. *I Will Lie Down This Night*. Chicago: Liturgy Training Publications, 1995.

O'Connell Killen, Patricia. *Finding Our Voices*. New York: Crossroad, 1997.

O'Murchu, Diarmuid. *Quantum Theology*. New York: Crossroad, 1997.

Prejean, Helen. "A Way out of No Way." *America* (August 29, 1998).

Ramshaw, Gail. *Words around the Table*. Chicago: Liturgy Training Publications, 1991.

Rohr, Richard, with John Bookser Feister. *Jesus' Plan for a New World*. Cincinnati: St. Anthony Messenger Press, 1996.

Rumi. *The Essential Rumi*. Trans. Coleman Barks with John Moyne. New York: HarperSanFrancisco, 1995.

Rupp, Joyce. *May I Have this Dance?* Notre Dame, Ind.: Ave Maria Press, 1992.

Shea, John. *Gospel Light*. New York: Crossroad, 1998.

Stone, Irving, ed. *Dear Theo: The Autobiography of Vincent van Gogh*. Garden City, N.Y.: Doubleday, 1937.

Unsworth, Tim. "Young Catholics." Special Spirituality Section. *National Catholic Reporter* (December 4, 1998).

Walker, Alice. *In Search of Our Mothers' Gardens*. San Diego: Harcourt Brace Jovanovich, 1983.

Yeats, William Butler. *Selected Poems and Two Plays of William Butler Yeats*. Ed. M. L. Rosenthal. New York: Macmillan, 1962.

Acknowledgments

The following selections by Kathy Coffey appeared originally in the publications listed below:

"A Canaanite's Terrain" in *Theology Today* and *St. Anthony Messenger*

"After the Annunciation" in *St. Anthony Messenger*

"Drumming the Rivers" in *Theology Today* and *St. Anthony Messenger*

"Well of Another Water" in *St. Anthony Messenger*

Parts of "Charcoal Fires" in *U.S. Catholic* under the title "The Host with the Most"

"Of Spirits and Spines," in *Theology Today* and *St. Anthony Messenger*

"Flying Carpet: Capernaum" in *St. Anthony Messenger*

"Lament of the Unpaid Mourner" in *St. Anthony Messenger*